PRACTICAL CHRISTIAN LIVING

by Wayne Taylor

THE WORD
FOR TODAY
P.O. Box 8000, Costa Mesa, CA 92628

Practical Christian Living
by Wayne Taylor
General Editor: Chuck Smith
Published by **The Word for Today**
P.O. Box 8000, Costa Mesa, CA 92628
(800) 272-WORD (9673)
http://www.thewordfortoday.org

© 1995 The Word for Today
ISBN 0-936728-57-5

Unless otherwise indicated, all Scripture quotations in this book are taken from the New King James Version of the Bible. Copyright © 1979, 1980, 1982 by Thomas Nelson, Inc., Publishers. Used by permission.

Verses marked NIV are taken from the Holy Bible, New International Version®. Copyright © 1973, 1978, 1984 by the International Bible Society. Used by permission of Zondervan Publishing House. The "NIV" and "New International Version" trademarks are registered in the United States Patent and Trademark Office by International Bible Society.

TABLE OF CONTENTS

Preface

When Luke wrote the message of the gospel to Theophilus, he declared that his desire was to set forth in order a declaration of those things that are most surely believed among us. Luke desired that Theophilus might know the certainty of those things in which he had been instructed.

We seem to be living in a day of spiritual confusion. Paul wrote to the Ephesians that they not be as children tossed to and fro with every wind of doctrine by the slight of men and the cunning craftiness whereby they lie in wait to deceive. Because of all the confusion in the church today, and the many winds of doctrine that continue to blow through the body of Christ, we felt that it would be good to have various pastors write booklets that would address the issues and give to you the solid biblical basis of what we believe and why we believe it.

Our purpose is that the spiritual house that you build will be set upon the solid foundation of the eternal Word of God, thus we know that it can withstand the fiercest storms.

Pastor Chuck Smith Calvary Chapel of Costa Mesa, California

Introduction

The life that Jesus Christ gives us is a life that works, and it works wonderfully! On the other hand, living apart from Christ in this cruel world, a person can easily be chewed up and left wasted.

The word "dysfunctional" has become a popular and overused term these days, but it is descriptive of so many lives that aren't working smoothly, purposefully, or productively. Modern society is often like a huge machine that is terribly defective, yet still cranks out product—tragically, that product is battered, broken, damaged people.

But Jesus fixes people, and according to John 10:10, he wants to give us an "abundant life." The life that Christ gives is meant to be lived out fully and functionally. The only truly fulfilling Christian life is being a "functional Christian"—that is, an active Christian, an involved Christian, a participant in the Body, a person enjoying and extending God's love.

I remember my very first cassette player was an old portable model. I loved that thing, taking it with me wherever I went. I used it for years, but I never cleaned it or did anything to maintain it. After a while it didn't play tapes, it ate tapes. Every single tape I put in, it would eat. It was very dysfunctional. Then one day, it was stolen out of my car. I was so happy. I was rejoicing! Now, I have a top-notch, deluxe model, "boom box" style cassette/CD player. It plays with such quality and smoothness. It is superbly functional.

This illustrates how Jesus transforms people from being worn out, "damaged goods," into being vibrant and productive children of God. "If anyone is in Christ, he is a new creation; old things have passed away; behold, all things have become new" (2 Corinthians 5:17).

This book is sort of a "how to" book: How to be superbly functional, fruitful Christians. Only God can tell us how, and through the Apostle Paul in Romans chapters 12 and 13, He does just that. *Practical Christian Living* is a commentary on those marvelous words.

Wayne Taylor Calvary Fellowship Seattle, Washington

CHAPTER 1
PRACTICAL CHRISTIAN LIVING

A few years ago, our family mini-van was in need of new tires, so I took a trip to the tire store. The salesman was so excited about tires. He went on and on about radials, steel belted, aluminum belted, aqua tread, and snow tires. He rambled for twenty minutes, even showing me newspaper clippings with pictures of tires. But after a while I'd had enough talking, so I said, "Let's get these tires on my van and see how they perform, because the proof of how good tires really are, begins 'Where the rubber meets the road.'"

The proof of real Christianity also begins, "Where the rubber meets the road." It's not just talking, but walking with the Lord. This is what's thrilling about Jesus Christ: when you walk with Him, He will handle the bumps and the corners of this world. He is there right down to the "tread" of our everyday lives.

Living Out Christianity

Throughout the book of Romans, Paul describes true Christianity by telling us about all the riches of relationship we can have with God, simply through trusting Jesus and receiving Him. In the first eleven chapters of Romans we find incredible doctrine, but Paul is never satisfied to just give us exalted truth. He begins with truth, but he always follows with practical application, calling us to live out those exalted principles.

Christianity isn't just a wonderful theory or philosophy. Jesus said, "I have come that they may have life, and that they may have it more abundantly" (John 10:10). The Christian life is an abundant life of knowing God and living for Him. Christianity is not a "spectator sport." It's being involved with Christ, being active, and giving Him 100 percent. I find this is where many Christians miss out. They love to hear about the riches of Christ, but they don't experience His riches in their daily lives. They are not presenting themselves each day to God, nor are they submitting their lives to Him. They are missing out on the awesome pleasure that can be found through putting themselves in His hands.

The Purpose For Our Lives

Christianity is not just going to meetings once a week, it's an everyday relationship— an exciting, active involvement. That is why Paul pleads with us in Romans 12:1,2, "I beseech you therefore, brethren, by the mercies of God, that you present your bodies a living sacrifice, holy, acceptable to God, which is your reasonable service. And do not be conformed to this world, but be transformed by the renewing of your mind, that you may prove what is that good and acceptable and perfect will of God." Here we have the supreme purpose for our lives as believers: we're to be living offerings, presenting ourselves to God each day.

Beyond just saying affectionate words of praise, we must present our bodies "a living sacrifice, holy, and acceptable," letting Him transform our minds, instead of letting our minds be conformed to this world. As we are transformed through presenting ourselves daily, we will know the "good and acceptable and perfect will of God." This is how we love God in a practical way.

"I beseech you..."

Paul begins Romans chapter 12 with, "I beseech you therefore, brethren, by the mercies of God..." "Beseech" is a good old fashioned word that is seldom used anymore. You don't hear it much around the office; your boss doesn't say, "I beseech you, quit goofing off"' Bosses generally use stronger language than that. But Paul doesn't use harsh language. Instead, he says, "I beseech you," which literally means, "to urge or invite." Paul is being gentle, though very earnest. This is how God speaks to us, "I appeal to you. Give Me your life because of My mercy towards you." The Lord doesn't demand that we submit. He doesn't want our response towards Him to be forced; He wants us to respond out of love.

"...by the mercies of God"

It's "by the mercies of God" that we are able to present our bodies to Him as living sacrifices; the word "by" meaning "through the agency of His mercies," or "by means of His mercies." In other words, through all the mercies God has given to us, we have all the means we could possibly need to live for Him. If you're a believer and have received the love of Christ, don't tell me you can't live for the Lord! He has given you His mercies so you can give yourself to Him.

All those mercies are to enable us to have motivation, ability, and strength to live for the Lord, and sacrificially present our bodies to Him. In Romans 6:13 we're commanded, "And do not present your members as instruments of unrighteousness to sin, but present yourselves to God as being alive from the dead, and your members as instruments of righteousness to God." Because as Christians you have the Holy Spirit, you have a choice. You don't have to "present yourself to sin." You can be an

instrument in the hands of the Lord, like a guitar
is an instrument in the hands of a master
musician. God is your Master, and He wants to
play beautiful music of love through you.

Present Your Bodies

You might have expected Paul to say,
"present your spirits." It's funny how spiritual
we can be sometimes, admonishing others to
"just give your spirit to God." Well, friend, your
spirit already belongs to God; what He really
wants is your body so He can put it to good use.
When you give your body to the Lord, you're
giving Him the "house" of your spirit and soul.
Your spirit already belongs to the Lord, you give
Him your body, He will transform your mind,
which is your soul, then *everything* will belong to
Him. Perhaps you're asking, "Why would He
want an evil body?" Our bodies are not evil. Our
flesh is evil, but that doesn't equate to our
bodies. The flesh is that principle of sin that
dwells in your bodies, but your body itself is not
sinful.

You might think your body is not that
important to God. Maybe you look at your body

and wonder, "Why would He want it? It's not really that beautiful or talented." It's precious to Him, because if you have trusted Christ, He has made that body of yours into His temple. Consider what Paul told the Corinthians, "Or do you not know that your body is the temple of the Holy Spirit who is in you, whom you have from God, and you are not your own? For you were bought at a price; therefore glorify God in your body and in your spirit, which are God's" (1 Corinthians 6:19,20). When we are talking about the laws of God's universe, legally, your body belongs to Him and it's illegal for you to use your body for purposes He didn't design it for. He wants your body to be a temple of worship—there should be service for Him going on within you. Worship doesn't go on only during the praise time at church, but worship happens everyday if you're putting yourself at His disposal.

Living Sacrifices

Under the Old Covenant, God required dead sacrifices. The sacrifice that corresponds to Romans 12:1 was the burnt offering, which was placed on the altar of God, then lit on fire. As it was consumed, a fragrant aroma went up to God. It's much like the meat you barbecue out in your backyard that smells so good you can hardly wait to eat it. The burnt offering was symbolic of the person giving his life completely to the Lord who could hardly wait to enjoy their service unto Him.

That was a dead sacrifice, but now God wants a living sacrifice. We're to be like the burning bush that Moses saw manifesting the Lord on Mt. Sinai. That bush caught Moses' attention because it was burning, but it wasn't destroyed or turned into ashes. Living wholly and continually for the Lord won't destroy you or burn you out. Instead, it will empower your life and attract attention because it's so rare. There aren't that many people who are really enthusiastic for the Lord in a solid and continual way. That's how God wants us to be, because He reaches people through our fervency and His presence filling our lives. Lives are ministered to through our enthusiasm for Him.

Holy Sacrifices

Along with being living sacrifices, Romans 12:1 calls us to be holy sacrifices. "Holy" in its Greek root means to be "set apart" or "sacred." The exact opposite of holy is not sinful or unclean, but "secular." The Latin word "secular" literally means "belonging to this world or age." As believers, we don't belong to this world, we're sacred, we belong to God. Jesus, in dying on the cross, made you sacred to God, setting you apart for Him. The struggle comes because God wants us to be in this world, but not of it. Most of us work in the secular realm, and all of us live in the secular realm, but God doesn't want us to be taken in by secular motivations and methods. We can have secular jobs, but in a sacred way, work out of love for Him and a desire to glorify Him. It is as if we had stamped on our backs, "Sacred: Not For Worldly Use."

The world wants to use you and abuse you—don't let it. If you get caught up in the greed, materialism, ambition, and lust of this world, you're going to be ground up like dog meat. But the Lord doesn't operate that way. As

He uses us and overflows our lives, we will be energized and blessed. We will have respect for ourselves, and respect for others.

The Logical Conclusion

So, we are to present our bodies, holy and acceptable. We're to be well-pleasing to God, which according to Romans 12:1 is our "reasonable service." The word "reasonable" means "logical." The most logical move you can make is to present yourself to God, because only what is done with and for the Lord is going to remain. When we stand before God, how much of our life is going to go up in smoke? And how much of it is going to remain as beautifully refined gold, silver, and precious stones? The Lord wants you to be a priceless treasure, and He wants you to lay up treasures, not only for His glory, but for your blessing. That's our calling, wherever we work, whatever our "lot in life," to be a sweet smelling sacrifice for Him.

Chapter II
Metamorphosis By The Spirit

In Matthew chapter 17, the transfiguration of Jesus is recorded: "Now after six days Jesus took Peter, James, and John his brother, led them up on a high mountain by themselves; and He was transfigured before them. His face shone like the sun, and His clothes became as white as the light." Jesus was transfigured temporarily into the form we will see when He comes again in His glorified state. His appearance was brilliant and dazzling, His face gleamed and glistened like the sun, and even His clothes shone out like a flood lamp with white light from within. Jesus was veiled in human flesh when He came as a man, but for a few moments, His inner glory was allowed to shine forth.

"Transfigured" is the same word translated "transformed" in Romans 12:2: "Do not be conformed to this world, but be transformed by the renewing of your mind, that you may prove what is that good and acceptable and perfect will of God." The transfiguration of Jesus portrays how we are transformed by letting His light dispel the darkness in our minds and moods, then shine out into our behavior: how we conduct our lives, and how we live our lives towards others. The Lord wants to transform carnality and selfishness, and give us new hearts. We won't start glowing in the dark or have a halo, but we will be changed on the inside so that outwardly we can shine forth His love, truth, and purity.

Metamorphosis

How can we make sure that we're not conformed to this world, but transformed by the renewing of our minds? In Greek, "transformed" is *metamorphoo*, from which we get "metamorphosis" meaning "a complete change of form." A classic example of metamorphosis is the growth and development of a frog. When frog eggs hatch, little fish-like creatures with long tails called tadpoles appear. Tadpoles must live in the water, but later they metamorphose into frogs, which can live in the water and on land. How does this change take place? Their thyroid gland produces hormones that control this process. Tadpoles need iodine to stimulate the growth of their thyroid, which secretes the chemical that allows them to turn into frogs. Without food containing iodine, the tadpole will keep growing, but he will never become a frog. Isn't that sad? He just becomes a huge tadpole! On the other hand, if the tadpole lives on food rich in iodine, he will change into a frog much quicker.

The Living And Powerful Word Of God

In our lives, the Holy Spirit is the One who uses the living water of Christ and the food of God's Word to transform us. If we're on a starvation diet in terms of taking in the Scripture, we will remain immature spiritually, and our minds will be directed by our own thoughts and ways, which are not God's ways. "For the Word of God is living and powerful, and sharper than any two-edged sword, piercing even to the division of soul and spirit, and of joints and marrow, and is a discerner of the thoughts and intents of the heart" (Hebrews 4:12). God's Word is able to cut away the things that are immature and hurtful to our spiritual walks. So, if we allow the Holy Spirit to minister God's Word to us by bathing our thoughts with the promises and the commands of Scripture, we're going to be changed much more rapidly and much more fully.

Have you ever wondered why some people grow as Christians much faster than others? They really take off, becoming stronger in their faith and used by the Lord. Then there are those who become Christians, but years later they haven't changed a bit. They still have the same old struggles and they're not really progressing much. I've observed this phenomenon for years, and I've concluded that it boils down to which people get into God's Word and let God's Word "get into" them. It makes all the difference when we cleanse our minds with the "washing of water by the word" (Ephesians 5:26).

Who Is Washing Your Brains?

We only have two choices in how we live our lives on this earth. We can either be conformed to the world, or be transformed by the Holy Spirit. These are the two awesomely powerful influences in the world today, and you're being molded by one of them. You really have no choice—there's no way to escape it. When people say to me, "Oh, you Christians, you're all brainwashed," I answer, "I grant you, I am brainwashed—I've chosen to let Jesus wash my brains. Who's washing your brains? And who's hanging them out to dry?" Basically, if you're not letting Christ wash your brains, then the world is soiling your brains. The world's conforming power is so great, unless the power of God is counteracting it, you are being conformed. The only way to be a "non-conformist" is to be transformed by God and by His Word.

Supernatural Forces Of Evil

The Bible teaches that behind the form and fashion of this age, there are horrible supernatural forces of evil. Ephesians 6:12

reveals, "We do not wrestle against flesh and blood, but against principalities, against powers, against the rulers of the darkness of this age, against hosts of wickedness in the heavenly places." Jesus called the devil the god and the ruler of this world, and "We know that we are of God, and the whole world lies under the sway of the wicked one" (1 John 5:19).

Do you think you're going to be the only one who has the power to resist? You're not. The devil and his spiritual minions use this world like a vise, squeezing people into its mold. Molding our minds into thinking that sensuality and immorality and materialism are the fulfilling and acceptable way to live. Telling us, "There are no absolutes, nor consequences in life. Therefore, live for yourselves and the pleasures of the moment!" To prove their point, they promote this lie with the most beautiful, witty, intelligent, and talented people. All this is to get you to love the world and the things in the world.

Without Christ, a person doesn't stand a chance of not being conformed to the world.

Even as Christians, we must stay on our guard. I don't watch a lot of television, but I do like to watch sports. Sometimes after watching a game, I'll find myself singing one of those catchy beer commercial jingles. My kids stop me and say, "Dad, did you know you're singing 'Glad to be your Bud'"? I feel so convicted by my own children! Now, I turn down the volume during the commercials.

No wonder the Apostle John warns us, "Do not love the world or the things in the world. If anyone loves the world, the love of the Father is not in him. For all that is in the world—the lust of the flesh, the lust of the eyes, and the pride of life—is not of the Father but is of the world. And the world is passing away, and the lust of it; but he who does the will of God abides forever" (1 John 2:15-17). Don't let your minds be flushed down the drain. With God's strength, we can go against the evil flow of this world because, "He who is in you is greater than he who is in the world" (1 John 4:4).

Priceless Treasures

By His power, we can swim upstream, though it is difficult and oppressive. As a Christian, you're going against the grain, but that's part of your commitment to Jesus, and it's worth it. Better to go against the flow to heaven than with the flow to hell! Actually, the Lord uses the world with all its trials, pressures, and hardships to do his wonderful work of transformation. Again, a great illustration of this can be found in nature in metamorphic rocks. These are rocks that change in form or re-crystallize, because of intensive heat and pressure. For example, through those means limestone can be changed into marble, and common carbon can be metamorphosed into diamonds. Limestone and carbon are not valuable, but marble and diamonds are worth a mint! But there must be intense pressure and heat before these rocks can become valuable. The Holy Spirit is seeking to change us into the priceless image of Christ, and He will use the pressures and pains the world inflicts upon us, in order to work a greater dependency deeply within our hearts, thus transforming us from dark ordinary carbon into bright costly diamonds.

Proving The Will Of God

Romans 12:2 goes on to explain why God transforms us: "that you may prove what is that good and acceptable and perfect will of God." "Prove" here means to "discern or discover." There are two steps to discerning God's will: 1. Present your body daily to God, and 2. Daily, resolve that God's Word, not the world, is going to mold your thinking. As you yield throughout the day, your life will become a beautiful unfolding of God's wonderful will.

I'm often asked, "How do you discover God's will for your life?" It's not hard. First thing each day, consistently say, "Here I am, Lord. I give you my life. I've got my schedule, but if you want to interrupt, please guide me. Program my mind with your Word, and rule my thoughts with your Spirit." As you do this, more and more your heart and mind will desire His ways and His wants. And as you read and listen carefully to the Scripture, you'll learn to hear His peaceful voice speaking to you, because His

Word is His voice. You will be able to sense the leading of His Spirit even in situations that are not specifically addressed in the Bible.

Written On Our Hearts

So often, we expect the Lord to direct us with miraculous signs—maybe we're looking for angelic sky writing, "Lord, if you would just write it in the sky, then I would know." Well, He is probably not going to do that, but Hebrews 8:10 says He will write His commands and laws upon our hearts and minds. As we delight ourselves in Him, He gives us the desires of our heart, and as we step out, we see His will unfold.

When my daughter was in the sixth grade, I was asked to coach her girls basketball team. At first, I declined because I have such a busy schedule. However, I wanted to be involved in her life, I like sports, and I know how to play, so I decided to go for it. It was amazing, not only the witnessing and discipling opportunities that arose with these girls, but almost every single game, I had adults approach me and say, "Aren't you that preacher, Wayne Taylor?" (they heard me yelling at the kids and recognized the voice!) Often times, they would share a great spiritual need with me. Many people came to the Lord or were built up in Him—I was shocked. God had simply placed His desires in my heart, then used the talents and gifts He had given me. While it seemed like I was taking a natural direction, in reality, He was leading me as I encountered people whom I never expected to, and opportunities that I didn't plan myself.

Frogs, Diamonds, and Butterflies

Allow me to conclude with one more nature illustration. At a certain point in time, a caterpillar will spin himself a little cocoon and just get quiet. I like to think of it as a little prayer closet where he gets alone before God and God does a work. You know what happens inside that cocoon? The caterpillar's life is literally melted into a liquid and completely reformed into another creature. When we come to the Lord, His Spirit starts working, and we're melted. Then, just like that cocoon will split open and a butterfly will flutter away, so we come out from being in God's presence, and His

Spirit has changed us. So many of us are crawling around like worms, day after day. How about taking a little time to get before the God of the universe and let His Spirit work in your heart and mind, empowering you to be different. Each and every day, "Do not be conformed to this world, but be transformed by the renewing of your mind, that you may prove what is that good and acceptable and perfect will of God."

Chapter III

Saved, Sane, and Sober Thinking

A young Englishman had just graduated from the famous Spurgeon's College, and had come to pastor his first church. On his first Sunday there, he stepped up into the pulpit filled with pride and confidence, thinking, "This congregation is so fortunate to have me as their pastor." But as he preached, he was having a very hard time of it, losing his place several times, stumbling over his words, and simply not communicating very well at all. He stepped down from the platform, noticeably distressed and brokenhearted. As he sheepishly stood by the door watching everyone file out, a wise old woman whispered to him, "Son, if you would have gone up into the pulpit the way you came

down, then you could have come down the way
you went up!"

In serving the Lord, nothing can put us on
the shelf faster than pride. Pride is a problem
today, and, judging from Paul's words, it must
have been a problem in his day: "For I say,
through the grace given to me, to everyone who
is among you, not to think of himself more
highly than he ought to think, but to think
soberly, as God has dealt to each one a measure
of faith" (Romans 12:3). Paul also said, "No
temptation has overtaken you except such as is
common to man"(1 Corinthians 10:13). Pride is
common to man—it's part of our fallen nature.
When we think of a proud person, we probably
envision someone who is blatantly boastful and
arrogant. But pride can take less obvious forms,
such as self consciousness, self-condemnation,
and self pity. Pride is an over concern with
self—it's the disease of "self-itus," and we're all
infected.

Saved Thinking

Pride is why Paul warns "everyone among
you, not to think of himself more highly than he

ought to think, but to think soberly..." Paul is making a play on words by using the word "think" four times, including the word "soberly" which means "to think with saved thinking." So, we could quote this verse, "You should not think of yourself more highly than you ought to think, but you should think with saved thinking." The essence of pride is thinking about yourself too much. Sadly, pride blinds our view of God. C.S. Lewis wrote, "A proud man is always looking down on things and people; and, of course, as long as you're looking down, you can't see something that's above you."

Proverbs 25:27 says it is not "a glory to seek one's own glory." There are two ways to seek our own glory. First, by telling ourselves how great we are, "Oh, that was such a wonderful speech I gave! Did you see the people gazing up at me?" But doing this is mimicking what the devil did in the beginning. He told himself, "I'm so much more glorious than all the other angels. I'm like God." Satan's prideful fall gives truth to this statement: "Humility makes men angels, but pride makes angels devils."

On the other hand, you can sit around and think about your glory in the sense that you don't have any, "I'm nothing. I'm scum. I'm a worm." Even though it's negative, your focus is still on yourself, and you're of no good to God when you do that—your effectiveness is short-circuited.

Sane Thinking

The problem of pride is found in our thoughts and in our minds. In the verse preceding Romans 12:3, Paul told us to "be transformed by the renewing of your mind." We are not going to change unless our minds are transformed and we start thinking soberly, or sanely, in regards to ourselves and serving the Lord. First, we must realize that any gift or ability we have comes from God. Paul asked the Corinthians, "What do you have that you did not receive?" (1 Corinthians 4:7). There is nothing we've received that God didn't give to us. He wants us to use what He has given to honor Him.

Romans 12:3 begins with "through the grace given to me..." Paul had received the grace of being an apostle, the foundational ministry within the body of Christ. The apostles were often used of God to do miracles and healings. Followers would look at them with glazed-over eyes and say, "You're so holy!" Acts 3:11,12 records, "Now as the lame man who was healed held on to Peter and John, all the people ran together to them in the porch which is called Solomon's, greatly amazed. So when Peter saw it, he responded to the people: 'Men of Israel, why do you marvel at this? Or why look so intently at us, as though by our own power or godliness we had made this man walk?'" Peter then goes on to explain that this man was healed, not by his own power, but through faith in Jesus Christ.

A Measure Of Faith

Paul concludes Romans 12:3, "God has dealt to each one a measure of faith." And according to Ephesians 4:7, we've also been given a measure of grace, a "dose of Jesus" with which to serve the body of Christ. You are an important part of the body, but all you have to give came from Him. We must also remember that there

are others who are gifted in the body; you're not
the only one, nor are you the most gifted one. To
realize that there are always going to be people
more gifted than us is sane thinking. Thank God
for these other people. Let them function and
know that as they serve the Lord, He is glorified
through them.

Sober Thinking

Pride is insane thinking, because truly, we
don't have anything to boast about. We should
only be boasting in the Lord, not in our flesh.
That's sober thinking. When we think of the
word "sober," we tend to think of "not drunk."
When you're drunk, you're not thinking
rationally; you're "under the influence."
Drinking gives people a false sense of
confidence. Often, a drunk guy will pick a fight,
thinking he is really tough—chances are he'll
end up with a broken nose! Or he might have a
sense of confidence about picking up women,
strutting around saying, "I'm quite the dude!",
making a fool out of himself.

That's what happens when you're drunk on
alcohol. We can also get drunk on pride. I once

read a funny story by C.E. Macartney: "After a minister had preached a searching sermon on pride, a woman who had heard the sermon waited upon him and told him that she was in much distress of mind, and that she would like to confess to a great sin. The minister asked her what the sin was. She answered, 'The sin of pride, for I sat for an hour before my mirror some days ago admiring my beauty.' 'Oh,' responded the minister, 'that was not a sin of pride—that was a sin of your imagination!'" A sense of self-glory can cause you to stop thinking clearly. Being consumed with self keeps you from thinking of yourself with God's thoughts. You might be thinking of yourself in some glorious fashion, but God's not. His desire is to glorify Christ. Or if you're beating yourself down with your thinking, those aren't His thoughts, either. The Lord wants you to turn to Him and realize that He loves you and values your life. You need to give Him your cares, quit dwelling on yourself, and start dwelling on Him.

Turn Your Eyes Upon Jesus

If you have either a false sense of glory or a false humility, take the words of this old hymn to heart, "Turn your eyes upon Jesus, look full in His wonderful face, and the things of earth will grow strangely dim, in the light of His glory and grace." Turn to Jesus and all that "self stuff" will be dispelled. An old Puritan once wrote, "The stars diminish when the sun comes up." Give Christ prominence by bringing pride and self-condemnation to the cross. Paul said, "I have been crucified with Christ; it is no longer I who live, but Christ lives in me" (Galatians 2:20). None of us are humble in our flesh, but that lowly, wonderful Spirit of Jesus living through us is the secret of humility.

In many of Jesus' statements recorded by John the apostle, we can see how perfectly He exemplified humility in His relationship with the Father: "The Son can do nothing of Himself" (John 5:19); "I do not seek my own will, but the will of the Father who sent Me" (John 5:30); "I do not receive honor from men" (John 5:41); "For I have come down from heaven, not to do My own will, but the will of Him who sent Me" (John 6:38); "My doctrine is not Mine, but His who sent Me" (John 7:16); "I have not come of Myself" (John 7:28); "I do nothing of Myself" (John 8:28); "I do not seek My own glory" (John 8:50); "The words that I speak to you I do not speak on My own authority" (John 14:10). Here is the Son of God, God the Son, saying "It's not Me. It's the Father." That's the secret for us: It's not me, it's Christ.

With a yielded attitude toward Christ, we can be used in any way He desires. Think of yourself as a slave of Christ. We're called to wait on people for Christ's sake, being at the disposal of Jesus and others. There is nothing glamorous about being a slave, unless we're doing it for the Master, then slavery is glorious!

Take A Look At Yourself

To determine if your thinking is saved, sane, and sober, ask yourself these questions: In whatever way you serve God, how do you see yourself? Is your ministry like a showcase for your gifts, or are your gifts merely an instrument pointing to Christ? Is the ministry a stepladder to something more? Do you find yourself thinking, "I can't do this, it's beneath me. I'm just waiting for the time when the Lord gives me a ministry that's worthy of me." When you're neglected or overlooked, how do you respond? How do you look at others as you minister? Do you see them as an opportunity to demonstrate your wisdom or display how mightily you can be used? Or do you see them as needy and loved by God? Are you willing to be interrupted, not just ministering to "important" people, but giving time to whomever God brings your way? How do you view people who minister to you? Are you "putting them on a pedestal," or are you giving God the credit for working through them?

Don't Bury Your Talents

Some people come up to me and say, "I can't be used by God. I'm just not gifted. I have nothing to offer the Lord." The truth is, you're wrong, so quit moping around! You're not "nothing," He's made you "something" and He wants to use you. To say, "I'm nothing," isn't being humble, it's calling God a liar. And calling God a liar isn't humble, it's *proud.*

God has given you grace and faith, so what are you doing with it? Are you using it? Are you stepping out and serving Him? Remember the Parable of the Talents. One guy had less talents than the others, but he did have a talent. He became afraid and buried it, and when his master came back, he said, "Master, here's your talent. You see, I didn't use it to gain anything because I was afraid, so I hid it." The master answered, "You wicked, lazy slave!"

Don't let your fears prevent you from stepping forth and being what God wants you to be. Cowardice and unbelief are sin. Take what the Lord has given you and as best you can, do something with it. You ask, "What should I do?" I don't know, just do it— anything! Check out the ministries your church offers. If one of them interests you, go for it. As you step out, the Lord will use you.

The other guys in that parable had two and five talents. They used them to get an equal number more, and when the master came back, he said to them, "Well done, good and faithful servant. You've been faithful with a few things. Enter into the joy of the Lord." Acknowledge that God has given you something. Take it and do whatever you can to multiply it. God will reward you as you glorify Christ with your life, because that's why you are here.

Chapter IV
You Belong To The Body

When you look at the human body, you see that it's a fabulous organism. The human body consists of 206 bones, over 600 muscles, 10 major organs and many minor ones, five quarts of blood, 60,000 miles of blood vessels, 50 trillion cells, and 300 trillion feet of DNA molecules, all jammed into a 20 square foot sheet of skin. But these statistics don't really describe a human, because the body is an awesomely connected whole. God didn't just throw together a bunch of DNA, random bones, muscles and so on, pour blood on it, wrap it in a sheet of skin and there it is—a big blob! Instead, He made the body a marvelous, connected, functioning unit, able to express a man or a woman's personality. The same is to be true of the parts of Christ's body. We're not to be a disconnected mass of unrelated members. Rather, we're to be joined together in love and service as a body through which Christ can express Himself in this world.

Members Of His Body

In Romans 12:4,5, we discover how the body of Christ is supposed to function, "For as we have many members in one body, but all the members do not have the same function, so we, being many, are one body in Christ, but individually members of one another." As Christians, we are members, first of all, of Christ—we belong to Him. But verse 5 says we also are "members one of another," and we belong to each other. One of the strongest drives within us is to feel like we belong. Yet, in today's society, it's difficult to quench that thirst for belonging. Generally, there's a gnawing sense in people that they don't fit anywhere, they feel alone and estranged. Our world is so cold, dangerous, and spiritually destructive.

In stark contrast, when we become members of the body of Christ, Jesus says, "You belong to

Me now." He becomes our Redeemer and
Master, and He promises, "I will never leave you
nor forsake you" (Hebrews 13:5). We're not our
own, we're not alone, and we belong to the most
special body of people in the world. The body of
Christ is the only body on earth who will never
breakup. Congress will disband, your crew at
work won't last forever, nor will your favorite
sports team, or rock band; even our marriages
and families won't be as they are now in heaven.
But the body of Christ will always be together
and we'll be married to Jesus as His bride
forever in eternity.

The Parts Of The Body

What are the main parts of the body of
Christ? First of all, there is one member of the
body who is vastly more important than every
other member: the head, Jesus Christ. We're told
in Ephesians 1:22, "And He put all things under
His feet, and gave Him to be head over all
things to the church." In other words, God put
Christ in charge of everything. Good choice. I
am so glad that God made Christ the head,
because He is the brains. In Him are hidden all

the treasures of wisdom and knowledge. When Jesus is directing every activity of His church, the body functions well—smoothly, effectively, in a coordinated fashion. But when He is not directing, the body suffers and becomes spastic and uncoordinated, and is not a true representation of Christ to the world.

Another supreme part of the body of Christ is the Holy Spirit. He is the nervous system, bringing messages and guidance from the brain to the body. From the day of Pentecost onward, the Holy Spirit has been the One empowering, directing, guiding, and building the body of Christ. As the church has come through the centuries, we've started saying, "Well, we have more knowledge now. We have great programs. We have computers!" Yet, after all these years, the most effective generation for doing the work of Jesus Christ was the first century church. They turned their world upside-down, while a significant percentage of our world has never heard of Jesus, even with all of our technologies. We've got to get back to looking to the Holy Spirit, for He is the One who empowers the body.

Then there is the body itself. All true believers who have received the Spirit of Jesus Christ are part of the body. Your church is a part of the worldwide body of Christ, along with the body of Christ that is already in heaven. A person's body is important and valuable to them. Think of all the time we spend on our bodies. Every morning, we probably spend a good hour or two getting out of bed, taking a shower, getting dressed, combing our hair, and eating our breakfast. Throughout the day, our tummy starts to rumble, so we feed it. You take care of your body. It's the same with Jesus. He nurtures and cherishes His body, and He loves to feed our spirits. He takes care of us because He wants us to be strong, coordinated, functioning, and healthy.

Many Members

In 1 Corinthians 12:17, Paul wonders, "If the whole body were an eye, where would be the hearing?" What if your body was just one huge eyeball? That would be weird—you'd be in the circus! We don't want the church to be a circus. To show forth God's love to the world through the church, it takes all the members working together. We learn in Romans 12:4 that there are "many members in one body," not just one member. Therefore, we need to appreciate and encourage *every* part of the body. Sometimes, it's the more needy and weak members who draw us together and help us realize that we belong to each other. The body is many members, and we need the variety and the fullness of every different member.

There is to be unity in the body, but not uniformity. As Paul says in verse 4, "though we have many members in one body, but all the members do not have the same function." Uniformity is not what the body of Christ is about, it's what cults are about. Cults are big on a uniform way of speaking and thinking. You can see them coming because they all look the same. This gives cult members the sense of identity they long for.

The Multi-Faceted Beauty Of Jesus

We Christians have found tremendous identity in Jesus. We are being conformed into the image of Christ, but His glory is so multifaceted that only by being who we are in our own unique way and all of us being different, can we represent the entirety of His beauty. If you try to be like me or if I try to be like you, a part of Christ's body won't be shining out. In becoming more like Christ, we're not necessarily going to become more like each other, except in the sense that well all become more holy and loving. Instead, our own human personalities will be expressed through the personality and the glory of God— His supernatural power working through natural people.

Don't be afraid to use your personality in expressing the truth, love, wisdom, and service of Jesus Christ. However, there is a danger here: Don't overemphasize your personality. Never should your personality ascend to the point where the message and glory of Jesus Christ are hidden. Our personality is only a vessel to communicate Him.

A Variety Of Gifts

There's an old saying, "Variety is the spice of life." Well, variety is also the spice of the body of

Christ. As we read on in Romans chapter 12, we
see that within the body, there is a variety of
gifts of the Holy Spirit, and 1 Corinthians 12 tells
us that our gifts produce a variety of effects.
"Effects" means that God determines the results
of our ministry. For example, even though two
of us are evangelists, our witness will have
different effects on the people we share with.
This gift will be expressed differently in each of
us in the way God has determined. For this and
other reasons, I must be careful not to
compare—I shouldn't think I'm unfruitful if I
don't have as many converts as they do.
Comparing only causes us to either become
prideful or become discouraged. Paul says
people who compare themselves with others are
"not wise" (2 Corinthians 10:12).

United In Christ

Though there is variety and multiplicity of
membership within the body, there is to be a
unity and a oneness. Three times in verses 4 and
5, Paul declares this oneness: "we have many
members in one body;" "we being many are one
body;" "individually members of one another."

The body of Christ is a great united organism, all for the purpose of glorifying and sharing Jesus Christ. We're not to be pulled every which way for different causes if they don't center on the person of Jesus Christ. As individual members, we're part of something much bigger than ourselves—so much bigger than any one of us, or even any group of us. As a member of Christ's body, my supreme goal is to function for the good of the whole, not for my personal good or gain. I'm not to be an independent "Lone Ranger," functioning for my own benefit. I am to be sacrificially serving and giving for the sake of everyone else and for the sake of Christ.

The Purpose Of Each Member

In a human body, every member functions for the good of the body. Actually, when cells begin to function for their own parasitic needs, they become very harmful to the body. This is how cancer cells behave—independent and out of control. The purpose of each member of a body is found in serving the body. Take your hands for example. Say you get hungry and your brain tells your hand, "Reach out and grab that burrito, put it in your mouth and feed the body." But what if your hand says, "I'm sick of feeding that body. He's always eating like a glutton. I'm going to slug him in the face instead!" That's no good. The hand's purpose has been negated and it's become harmful to the body—not a blessing at all! It's the same with your feet. What if the brain said, "Go over to the grocery store." So one foot starts going that way, but the other foot says, "No. I'm going to the park." The body's divided and it could be torn right down the middle.

These silly examples illustrate that the body of Christ can't be fruitful and effective unless each member is functioning and serving for the good of the whole and for the health of the body. In our human bodies, we have white blood cells. If an infection comes into the body, the white blood cells come and surround that infection and load it up with chemical explosives. They absorb that infection, then they blow it up and it's gone. In the process, they sacrifice themselves in order to serve the body. What a blessing—they should receive an award. Don't be afraid to serve the body sacrificially.

"We know love by this, that He laid down His life for us," and we ought to lay down our lives for our Christian brothers and sisters (1 John 3:16).

We need you to serve Christ in the body, and to consider it an honor to work together for the glory of our Lord. Every member is important. You are important, so get employed! If the body had 100 percent employment, we could be much more effective for Jesus. He longs to see us working together and appreciating each other.

Every Part Is Important

Once a great conductor gathered 200 accomplished musicians together to form an all-star symphony orchestra. As they were rehearsing a crescendo, suddenly the conductor stopped everything and asked, "Where's the piccolo?" Well, the piccolo player had figured he wasn't important and no one would notice if he took a break. But even during that tremendous crescendo, the conductor hadn't heard the little piccolo, because he had been listening for every part. The piccolo player thought his instrument was no big deal, but the conductor had missed it. That describes Jesus. I believe He is saying to many of us, "Where's the piccolo?" or, "Where's the kazoo?" Whatever it is, get it out and use it. Whatever you can do for the Lord, however you can serve the body, step up to the plate and He will bless it.

CHAPTER V
MOTIVATIONAL GIFTS IN THE BODY

I remember watching my dad shave when I was a kid. I would look up at him longingly, wishing I had whiskers. As he was standing there with his shirt off and his muscles bulging, I would compare my little biceps with his and say, "Dad, show me your muscles." He would flex his big arm, and I would compare it with my little piece of spaghetti! I was just a boy, but I wanted to be a man. I wanted to be big and strong—I wanted to grow up.

The goal of the Holy Spirit for our lives is spiritual maturity—to grow us up to be like Jesus. That maturity comes through feeding upon a good diet of God's Word, as well as exercising our part in the body of Christ. As we are equipped with the Word and we willingly step out to minister to one another, the gifts God has given cause us to become more like Christ. Jesus said, "For even the Son of Man did not come to be served, but to serve, and to give His life a ransom for many" (Mark 10:45). Serving was His purpose, and He wants us to serve as well, so He equips us to serve by giving each of us gifts of His Holy Spirit.

The Power Of The Spirit

In Romans 12:6, we are introduced to this topic of the gifts of the Spirit. The word "gifts" is *charismata*, which refers to endowments of power, wisdom, and grace that enable us to serve others in the body, serve the community, and glorify God. Today's church is often ineffective for Christ because we've neglected the power of the Holy Spirit that energized the early church. We've substituted programs for power, gimmicks have taken the place of the gospel, and perspiration has replaced inspiration. But these are no substitutes. With that dynamic power of God's Spirit, Acts 17:6 says the early church "turned the world upside-down," and it only took them 25 years to do it!

A.W. Tozer once said, "If the Holy Spirit was taken away from the early church, 90 percent of what they did would come to a screeching halt. But if the Holy Spirit was taken away from today's church, 90 percent of what we do would carry on without interruption." I find that a sad commentary. The church of today at large is not seeing the same fruit as the early church because we're not relying on the same power. We can't rely on our power or our wisdom, our ingenuity, or our programs. We need the power of God!

The Gifts Of The Spirit

This list of gifts found in Romans 12:6 8 is just one list among many found in the New Testament. Though there are only seven spiritual gifts listed here, there are many more listed elsewhere. Yet, this list is particularly important and vital within the body of Christ because these are what Pastor Jon Courson calls, "The Motivational Gifts of the Holy Spirit."

Which of these gifts you have will determine how you are motivated in serving the Lord.

Ephesians 4 is another passage that talks about the gifts of the Holy Spirit. In that section, Paul says, "but, *speaking the truth* in love, may you grow up in all things into Him who is the head—Christ" (Ephesians 4:15). As we examine this list in Romans 12:6-8 I would like to look at how these gifts motivate us in *speaking the truth.* Also, as we look at each one of these gifts, I will give an example from the life of Jesus Christ, because Jesus exemplified each gift perfectly.

Prophecy - Proclaiming Truth

Verse 6: "Having then gifts differing according to the grace that is given to us, let us use them; if prophecy, let us prophesy in proportion to our faith..." Prophecy is proclaiming truth. It's saying the Word "like it is," cutting through the rhetoric, piercing past and through the human barriers and forth telling the truth, pure and simple. Prophecy can also be foretelling truth: predicting the consequences that will result from a person's choices.

We see Jesus exercising this motivational gift of prophecy in Matthew 11. There, He starts out rebuking unbelievers from particular cities around Galilee where most of His mighty works had been done: "Woe to you, Chorazin! Woe to you, Bethsaida! For if the mighty works which were done in you had been done in Tyre and Sidon, they would have repented long ago in sackcloth and ashes. But I say to you, it will be more tolerable for Tyre and Sidon in the day of judgment than for you" (Matthew 11:21,22). Jesus is speaking as a mighty prophet. These people refused to listen earlier to His good news, so now He is piercing through with a message of judgment. He told them, "You're doomed," and consequently, these cities have vanished. There's a predictive nature here—Jesus is saying, "Because this is the way you're going, this is the way you're going to end up."

Later, in Matthew 11:28-30, Jesus uses the same gift of prophecy, but the other side of it. To the people who have tender, believing hearts and want to hear what He has to say, He proclaims, "Come to Me, all you who labor and are heavy-laden, and I will give you rest. Take My yoke upon you and learn from Me, for I am gentle and lowly in heart, and you shall find rest for your souls. For My yoke is easy, and My burden is light."

Jesus really cut through to the truth with this gift of prophecy. Do you have that kind of desire? Do you love to tell people the truth of what Jesus would say to them, or how He feels about them, or how He feels about a particular attitude? If you have the gift of prophecy, it will grow as you step out in faith and use it according to the proportion of your faith. As God uses you, your faith will grow, and the punch of your ministry will grow as well.

Serving - Illustrating Truth

Verse 7: "...or ministry, let us use it in our ministering..." The gift of service is illustrating truth; showing how the truth works in serving others. This gift is also called "helps" in 1 Corinthians 12:28. In the Greek it's the word *diakonia*, from which we get "deacon" or "deaconess," referring to someone who serves people in their practical needs. No matter what needs to be done, these people love to pitch-in and help. This is such a vital ministry within a church, because every Sunday, hundreds of servants are needed so people can listen to one preacher.

In Acts 9:36-42, we find the story of a woman named Tabitha who "was full of good works and charitable deeds which she did." When Tabitha became sick and died, her friends sent for Peter and showed him all the wonderful clothes she had made, and told him of all the things she had done for them.

Basically, they pleaded with Peter, "We need this gal, we can't afford to lose her! Please, do something!" So Peter said, "Tabitha, arise!", and she rose from the dead. When Peter set Tabitha before them, they were so excited— oh, how they had missed her service! No where in the Bible does it say that people missed preachers so badly they wanted them raised from the dead, but this servant Tabitha was missed because she had such an important ministry to them.

Jesus portrayed servanthood so beautifully. The night before He was betrayed, He took off His outer garments, wrapped Himself with a towel, took a basin, and washed the disciples' feet. He cleaned them and refreshed them. In those days, washing the feet of those who had been walking along the dusty roads was a real ministry of servanthood.

How we need people to illustrate what it is to live according to this truth, to be a servant. This gift of service is a supernatural ministry from God no less than teaching, prophesying or healing. These are people who don't want any recognition or big reward, they just want to use the practical abilities that God has given them to illustrate the truth.

Teaching - Explaining Truth

Verse 7: "...he who teaches, in teaching..." Teaching is explaining the truth. Someone who is gifted by God to take the Scripture and expound, clarify, and make it alive to its hearers. Jesus did this with the Old Testament. In Matthew 5:27,28, Jesus said, "You have heard that it was said to those of old, 'You shall not commit adultery.' But I say to you that whoever looks at a woman to lust for her has already committed adultery with her in his heart." Jesus is clarifying that when God gave us this Old Testament commandment, "You shall not commit adultery," He meant far more than just having an affair with a married person. Jesus was the best teacher who ever lived—and He still is. His parables, for example, clarify truth for all those who have ears to hear.

In 2 Timothy 3:16, Paul says *"all* Scripture is profitable." So, if you feel that you are called to be a spiritual teacher in the body, you must also have a great desire to study *all* of the Bible. This is how it became clear to me that God wanted me to teach His Word. Suddenly, I had a ravenous appetite to study the Bible. I couldn't get enough of it—I would study for hours and hours a day. After a while, the Lord led me to share with others what I had learned. Paul also told Timothy, "Be diligent to present yourself approved to God, a worker who does not need to be ashamed, rightly dividing the word of truth" (2 Timothy 2:15). It's just like a skilled surgeon who expertly uses a scalpel. If I'm going to be operated on, I really don't want someone who doesn't know which organ is which. The Lord wants teachers to know His Word before they minister His truth by explaining it to the body.

Exhortation - Stimulating Truth

Verse 8: "...he who exhorts, in exhortation..." Exhortation is stimulating truth, or stirring people in the truth. This is a vitally needed gift to help people apply the Word, get busy, and do what the Bible says. It's a complement to teaching: Teaching without exhortation produces fat and lazy sheep, but exhortation without teaching produces scrawny, undernourished, weak sheep. Hebrews 10:24,25 says, "Let us consider how to stimulate one another to love and good deeds, not forsaking the assembling of ourselves together as is the habit of some, but exhorting one another all the more as you see the day drawing near." I thank the Lord for the exhorters in the body because I'm really motivated by them. When someone stands up and says, "You guys get with it!", I feel excited! It makes me want to get going, like a spiritual "kick in the pants."

The other side of exhortation is comforting and consoling. For example, the mourners were crying and weeping at Lazarus' tomb, and Jesus came along and wept with them. But then He said to Martha, "Did I not say to you that if you would believe you would see the glory of God?" (John 10:40). He was exhorting her to "believe," but He was doing it in an encouraging way. Jesus also exhorted Lazarus inside the grave when He cried out in a loud voice, "Lazarus, come forth!" Lazarus obeyed, hobbling out of the tomb in his mummy clothes.

In a spiritual sense, exhorters raise the spiritual dead. They exhort and wake us up, and we respond, "Thanks, I needed that!" Exhortation also has its soft, comfort-oriented side. Hebrews 3:13 tells us to exhort one another day after day, "lest any of you be hardened through the deceitfulness of sin." We need exhortation—appreciate those among you who have this gift.

Giving - Supporting Truth

Verse 8: "...he who gives, with liberality.." Giving is supporting the truth. It is seen in people who are either gifted at making or saving money, and love to share that money to support the cause of Jesus Christ. These people are channels of God for funds and resources to further the propagation of God's work. Jesus was the ultimate giver. As it says in 2 Corinthians 8:9, "For you know the grace of our Lord Jesus Christ, that though He was rich, yet for your sakes He became poor, that you through His poverty might become rich."

Giving is a great gift, because furthering the cause of Christ does take material resources. We can all exercise this gift, yet there are some people who are especially blessed in this way. Verse 8 says to give "with liberality," which means "liberally, with no strings attached." Jesus said, "Don't sound the trumpet when you give alms" (Matthew 6:2). The Pharisees actually had little trumpets hooked to their robes. Whenever they were going to do a benevolent deed, they would blow their little horn. Then they would do their act of charity and everyone would be impressed. It's just like politicians today; whenever they're going to do something great, they call a press conference. But we're not to be like that. Give as unto the Lord, and the Lord will reward you.

Leading - Exemplifying Truth

Verse 8: "...he who leads, with diligence..." This gift of leadership exemplifies the truth. It is also called the "gift of administrations" in 1 Corinthians 12:28. Jesus, of course, was the consummate leader. For example, when He fed the 5,000, He told the disciples, "Give these people some food," but they whined, "We don't have enough! Don't you realize how much money it would take to feed all these people?" Jesus answered, "Feed them," and then explained to them how to do it. Jesus told the disciples to take the people, divide them up, put them in groups of fifty, etc., etc. That's how the gift of organization and administration works. Leaders don't see the impossible. They don't say, "Oh, we could never do that!" No, leaders say, "We can do it, and we will do it," then they get

busy and start managing. This gift is important
within the body of Christ which needs structure,
in order to make sure people are cared for and
don't "fall through the cracks." However, there
shouldn't be too much structure, just enough to
serve and meet the needs of the body.

Mercy - Demonstrating Truth

Verse 8: "...he who shows mercy, with
cheerfulness." Showing mercy is demonstrating
the truth. These are people who have a
tremendous sensitivity from God. They love to
weep with those who weep, and they have an
understanding heart. Jesus expressed this gift of
compassion at Lazarus' funeral. He knew He
was going to raise Lazarus from the dead, but
He still wept with the mourners when He saw
them in their sorrow. The Scriptures also record
that He felt compassion for the multitudes
because they were like sheep without a
shepherd, and He felt love in His heart for the
rich young ruler.

Those who have this gift are so wonderful to
have around, especially when you're hurting. At
those times, you don't really want a prophet,

you want someone to show you mercy. They will come to soothe and comfort you, and they minister to your broken heart.

Seven Different Motivational Gifts

Each one of these seven different gifts motivate us in how we will minister truth to others. Which one do you have? Maybe you have more than one, but one will be predominant. This gift will determine how you will react and how you will serve in a given situation.

Let me illustrate: Let's suppose I'm preaching on a Sunday morning and Robert, one of my assistant pastors, decides to get me a glass of water. But as Robert is coming down the aisle with the glass of water, he trips, breaks the glass, and water goes everywhere. How would you respond to Robert? If you were a prophet, you would proclaim truth saying, "Robert, my son. Be careful how thou walkest, for there are many stumbling blocks, sayeth the Lord." If your gift was service, you would say, "Let's get a broom and mop," and you'd pitch in to clean the mess up. But if your gift was teaching, you'd say, "Robert, when you're walking down the aisle, you've got to lift your feet a certain distance from the ground, because that rug has fiber that is very blunt.

And "blunt" in the Greek is the word *stumbeleko.*" If your gift was exhortation, you would say, "Robert, you klutz! You know better than that. Get up! Walk straight next time!" If your gift was giving, you'd say, "Let me replace that broken glass, and if you hurt your ankle, I'll pay the doctor's bill." If your gift was leading, you'd say, "Wayne, come here. Help me pick up Robert. Kim, go get a broom. Cathy, get a mop." If your gift was mercy, you'd say, "Oh, Robert, my dear. Are you all right? You must feel terrible. Come here and cry on my shoulder."

Does this humorous example help you see why we need such a wide variety of gifts? God gives these gifts so we can become more like Christ in our own way, and serve however He has given to us to serve. You're getting involved is so needed to bring about that full picture of Jesus Christ in the body. Sometimes we're afraid to step out because we might fail, or we feel like we don't have much to offer. But when you step out, God will help you. I encourage you, don't be afraid. What you are is someone the body needs!

Chapter VI
Exercising Your Body Part

It's fun to watch babies grow and develop. When a baby is a newborn, for instance, he is unable to feed himself. But when he becomes a toddler, he can start learning to use a spoon. So, we set little Johnny in his highchair and put a bowl of creamed cereal in front of him. At first, he keeps missing his mouth, getting cereal all over his face and in his hair. You might even put a big plastic bib on him to catch all the droppings, but most of his lunch will still end up on the floor. Now, you could feed Johnny for the rest of his life, but somewhere along the line, he needs to learn and it's bound to be messy. But eventually, with lots of practice, he will get his hand and mouth working together. You see, all the potential for productive use has been given to our body parts, and as we exercise them, they become strong and able to accomplish a variety of tasks.

Discovering Your Best Fit

God has given, or He will give you, gifts of the Holy Spirit. So the potential is there, but you must begin to step out and exercise those gifts. At first, it can be unclear or confusing as to which gifts are yours. You ask yourself, "How do I fit?" or, "Where can I serve?" You might feel uncoordinated, but as you open your life to the Spirit and make yourself available to Him, you will begin to find out what gifts He has given you, along with which ones He hasn't given you. In this way, you learn, you grow, and you become a very effective, fruitful member of the body of Jesus Christ.

There Is Beauty In Variety

In Romans 12:6, Paul says we have gifts *"differing* according to the grace that is given to us..." Within the body of Christ, variety is such a blessing—thank God we don't all have the same function! The reason rainbows are so striking is because of the beautiful blend of different colors. But what if the whole world and everything in it was one color? What if everything was green? That would be so blah! Most plant life is green, but m any different shades of green. Yet, though there are all these greenish hues, they all match! Man made greens usually don't blend, but the greens God made blend perfectly. It's the same in the body of Christ. There is a great variety that is meant to blend together, so the whole beauty of Christ can stand out.

Charisma

In this verse, the Greek word for "gifts" is *charisma*, from which we get the term "charismatic." When we say someone has "charisma," we mean they really stand out and attract our attention. In a general sense, when God gives you a spiritual gift, he puts some "charisma" into your function as a human being and that gift becomes a very attractive aspect of your life. He is giving you a spiritual dynamic, even beyond the natural dynamic that He gave you when He made you. This doesn't mean people will begin mistaking you for a glamorous movie star, but gifts of the Spirit will add a dynamic new dimension to your life.

Charis

Charisma comes from the same root word as the word for "grace," which is *charis,* meaning "a free gift of God's favor." This refers to a divine enablement that God gives us as a favor—a "Holy Spirit gratuity" given according to God's grace. Ephesians 4:7 says, "But to each one of us grace was given according to the measure of Christ's gift." Christ gave His whole life, and according to that measure, He has given out many "graces." This verse is not talking about grace for salvation, but grace for service. According to 1 Corinthians 12:7, "The manifestation of the Spirit is given to each one for the profit of all." God gives you the power of the Spirit to manifest God's reality through your life to others. Each and every person receives grace and gifts from God in order to function in the body and manifest His presence. So, God wants you to step out and use what He has given you.

Chairo

It's very interesting to me that the word *charisma* and the word *charis* both come from a deeper root, *chairo,* meaning "to be cheerful and joyful." We all know that receiving God's grace is a great joy. It's such a pleasure to have His love, favor, and blessing upon your life. *Charisma* is derived from this word because using what God has given you to serve others will make you cheerful. When you are doing what God made you spiritually to do, it's not a drudgery, but a joy. Jesus said, "Take my yoke upon you... for my yoke is easy and my burden is light" (Matthew 11:29,30). Using your spiritual gift is easy because He has empowered you and it's very natural because that's how God has made you. You find yourself thinking, "This is what the Lord wants me to do. This is my life."

A Laughing Revival?

Joy and cheerfulness come from being a vessel touched and used by the Spirit in serving God. It's not merely a "happiness from heaven," or an ecstatic experience. We can have great experiences with God that are very emotionally touching, but that's not where the deep joy is found. I bring this out because there are people today who are primarily seeking these ecstatic experiences. For example, many are involved in a movement called "The Laughing Revival" or "The Toronto Blessing." During their meetings, they become overwhelmed with hysterical laughter. Some jerk and writhe on the floor, and many others make animal noises such as barking, growling, roaring, and chirping. This goes on even during the message. The whole atmosphere is chaotic and confusing, and very much "hyped" by the leader.

In 1 Corinthians 14:32, Paul said, "And the spirits of the prophets are subject to the prophets." In other words, God doesn't come on us in such a way that we're totally out of control and we "can't help ourselves," but that is what the Holy Spirit is being accused of doing. No, when the Holy Spirit is working, there is order and peace. If you are truly manifesting spiritual gifts, you will have more self-control, not less, because self-control is a fruit of the Spirit.

We can experience God in joyful and even ecstatic ways when we are filled with His Spirit. I encourage you to wait before the Lord and let Him bless you. Some of us, quite honestly, probably need to loosen up a bit. But keep in mind, Paul also said, "God is not the author of confusion but of peace, as in all the churches of the saints... Let all things be done decently and in order" (1 Corinthians 14:33,40). Worship is to be decent and orderly, not chaotic and hysterical. We must follow the guidelines of Scripture, otherwise people will overreact emotionally to what the Holy Spirit is doing, and their reactions will become a distraction. God fills and gifts us to serve, and this is where the greatest joy lies—being what He has made you to be.

I love what Warren Wiersbe said about the gifts of the Holy Spirit, "They are not toys to play with. Nor weapons to fight with. But tools from God to build with." How true that is. You find in some places people using the gifts like toys, "Hey, let's have some fun!" Nor are spiritual gifts an issue to battle over and argue about. They're tools for the believer to bless one another. Each of us as members of Christ's body need to step out and utilize the grace and the gifts that God has given us. This is how we grow and mature, and this is how the body builds itself up, matures, and grows as well.

Spiritual Exercise

"Having then gifts differing according to the grace that is given to us, let us *use* them," or, "let us *exercise* them" (Romans 12:6). We all know that being active is important. In recent years, we've learned that exercise can positively effect your health. In fact, living a sedentary life without any vigorous physical exercise, activity, or labor can lead to some serious health problems. This is especially true as we get older. When we're young, it seems we can get away with eating anything we want. But then there comes a time in our early thirties when we've got to stop eating so much! At that point, we'd better start exercising, or we're going to change shape. That hour-glass turns into an upside-down pear as our muscle tone begins to deteriorate. A slippage takes place, what one of my friends calls "a polar axis shift."

There's a real danger for those of you who have known the Lord for a long time and consider yourselves knowledgeable in Scripture. As 1 Corinthians 8:1 states, "Knowledge puffs up, but love edifies." When I read this verse, I picture someone taking in all kinds of knowledge, saying, "Feed me, feed me!" But then, they become bloated because they are not using this knowledge in sacrificial service. On the other hand, I can also picture someone taking it all in, being well-fed, then using and exercising what they have learned.

They become finely tuned and strong, able to function like a professional athlete.

Beware of Withdrawing From Spirituality

Often, the lives of older Christians become complicated. We get married, have kids, develop our careers, and so on. These are not bad life changes, but they do add more and more stress to our lives. As this happens, the tendency is to withdraw from receiving spiritually. When we're too busy, the first thing to go is usually our commitment to give and serve. Consequently, we start sitting on the sidelines, criticizing those who are doing the job, thinking, "They're not doing it quite right. After all, I know what the Bible says." A pridefulness develops, and that's not good.

Now, I realize there needs to be a balance. God wants us to spend lots of quality time with our friends, spouses, and children. But as our lives change, we must not withdraw from being actively involved in the body, because our friends and families need to see us serving. This is what sharpens our spiritual edge and keeps us from becoming spiritually obese and incapable of being fruitful for the Lord. I pray that the Lord would help us to heed Paul's exhortation and *use* as best we can, what God has given us. When we stand before His Judgment Seat, it will be music to our ears to hear, "Well done, good and faithful servant."

CHAPTER VII
OUR TRADEMARK IS LOVE

Let's suppose you go to a restaurant and order a bowl of clam chowder. You can hardly wait because you are really hungry and you *love* clam chowder. The waitress comes up and puts before you a beautiful china bowl. Inside the bowl with fancy lettering it says -*Clam Chowder*~ but the bowl is empty! You tell the waitress, "I don't see any clam chowder in there." She answers, "Yes, but isn't it a lovely bowl?" You respond, "It looks nice, but it won't nourish me. So, could you just get me a plain bowl filled with clam chowder?"

Nourished With Love

Within the body of Christ, it's God's love that nourishes and satisfies. His love is what really "hits the spot" and fills our hearts. You might be supplying a beautiful ministry, but without love, it will be empty and cold. Love is the circulatory system of the body of Christ. The heart, Jesus Christ, longs to pump His love into you, so that you can become an artery, vein, or capillary bringing His love out to the very tips of His fingers. Without love, a church body soon becomes a lifeless corpse. Have you ever been in a dead church? There's not much warmth there because the love has dissipated. Somehow, God's love isn't getting through.

In the second chapter of Revelation, Jesus warned the church of Ephesus that He would remove His presence unless they repented of being loveless. They may have had great teaching, but Jesus said, "I have this against you, that you have left your first love." Jesus will not stay in a loveless church. We are called to be the body of Christ, not the cadaver of Christ. Not cutting, dissecting, biting, and devouring one another, but nurturing and caring. Jesus Christ is risen and alive, and we too need to be alive with the love of God. We can discover what this love is to look like through a careful study of Romans 12:9-13.

Agape

Romans 12:9,10: "Let love be without hypocrisy. Abhor what is evil. Cling to what is good. Be kindly affectionate to one another with brotherly love, in honor giving preference to one another..." These verses contain three different Greek words for love. The first one, "Let love be without hypocrisy," is *agape*. Agape love is selfless, sacrificial, unconditional love. In and of ourselves, we can't give agape love. I'm not saying you can't be sacrificially loving, but without receiving Jesus Christ's pure, unconditional love, you can never love in a totally unselfish way. Only Christ loves with absolute, selfless perfection. We all long to be loved perfectly by someone who cares more about us than themselves, and the Lord wants to supply our need for this love. He doesn't need to be taken care of, so He can concentrate His effort and time on caring for us. As God fills us with His love, we're able to give His love to others.

At times, agape love will require great cost and pain. Remember, the greatest demonstration of agape love was on the cross where Jesus laid down His life. The opposite of love is not hate, it's selfishness, and agape love requires the sacrifice of self. We must take our selfishness to the cross and receive the identifying brandmark of love: the nail prints of Christ. When I was a kid, I would watch my grandfather brand horses with a hot iron. Those horses were smarting as the brand sizzled their hides, but after the pain subsided, that brand looked handsome on them, and it would provide protection from horse thieves.

In the same way, the agape love of Christ looks good on you. People are amazed when they see His brand of loving and giving in someone. It is a very attractive, unique, and unselfish love. His love also protects us from the great thief, Satan. Jesus said, "The thief does not come except to steal, and to kill, and to destroy. I have come that they may have life, and that they may have it more abundantly" (John 10:10). The devil wants to steal the riches of Christ from us, and he uses our selfishness to rob us of the blessings the Lord has for us.

Phileo

The Greek word *phileo is* used twice in verse 10, "Be kindly *[phileo]* affectionate to one another with brotherly love *[philadelphia]...*" Phileo is a fondness, a kindness, or a friendship-oriented love. Jesus' disciples were friends because they "hung out" together. They enjoyed being with each other, as well as being with Jesus. You must realize that these guys came from different backgrounds, yet they became "best buds." They loved the Lord, they shared the Lord, and they served the Lord. This is what bonds hearts together: sharing together in what God has done in our lives, and ministering to others together.

Sometimes we criticize the disciples because they argued. But, a sign of brotherly love is when you can argue without losing your love and commitment. Generally, you wouldn't start an argument with a stranger. Even if they make an "off the wall" statement, you don't respond,

"That was so stupid!" But with a family member, you don't hesitate to give your opinion! You've got that freedom because you love each other. Likewise, you can't overly tease someone you've just met because they might not understand. But it's fun to tease our relatives and our friends! You do need to oil this kind of communication with assurance, kindness, and tenderness, because you don't want to drive a wedge between you. As you build relationships within the body, don't think, "Oh, I can't be honest. I don't want to upset the apple cart." Go ahead—tell your brothers and sisters in Christ what you're thinking. They need to hear how you feel, even though they may not always like it!

Storgoia

Another word for love is used in verse 10, "Be kindly affectionate..." The word "affectionate" in the Greek is *storgoia* which means "family love, affection, or devotion." Family members are usually devoted to one another. They may not like each other very well, but they're family. If a need arises, they are there for you; even if they're busy, they make time. My brother Kelley is very gifted at handiwork—he's a carpenter, a plumber, he does it all. I don't. I remember a few years back, we had a leaky sink. While I was trying to repair it, my wife called Kelley. He came right over and fixed it. He was busy, but he took pity on me.

Because Kelley is my blood brother, we have a real bond. Within the body, we're bonded together by the blood of Jesus Christ. His redeeming blood has tied us together supernaturally as brothers and sisters. Let's have a family's heart about meeting needs—especially towards single parents and their kids, those who don't have relatives near by, and those who can't take care of themselves.

Give Preference And Honor

At the end of verse 10, Paul sums up his teaching by defining love: "in honor giving preference to one another." An alternate reading of this verse is, "out-do each other in showing honor to the other." In the early days of our marriage, my wife Cathy and I had a hard time giving preference to one other. When we were first married, we tended to want to protect our place, making sure we weren't taken advantage of or hurt. We guarded our territory, thinking we'd better keep something for ourselves, "just in case."

When Cathy and I came across this verse one day, we decided, "If we have an argument, let's see who can 'out-do' the other, give-in and say, 'I'm sorry' first." So, we had this competition going and Cathy kept winning! Prior to this, I didn't realize how selfish I was, but now that I was losing, I could see that I was not giving preference and honor to my wife. The Lord showed me, "You can repent when you're selfish, and I will change you." And He has changed me—just ask my wife! I haven't arrived, I still need to repent *a lot*, but through conscious repentance, unconscious love is growing.

Evil Versus Good

So that our love is not hypocritical, Paul tells us to "abhor what is evil. Cling to what is good" (verse 9). The message you often hear in the media is, "Love is how you *feel.*" But true love is not Hollywood love. Love hates evil, and love is not morally weak. Love is filled with goodness and acts of kindness, and is completely devoid of wickedness. Evil hurts your relationship with God and it hurts your ability to love others. 1 John 5:2 explains, "By this we know that we love the children of God, when we love God and keep His commandments." We're really loving our fellow brothers and sisters when we don't allow evil to compromise our walks with God. This is a good example and encouragement to our fellow believers. God can help us abhor evil and cling (literally in Greek, alike glue") to what is good.

How To Share Love

Paul concludes this section by listing several ways love is to be shared: "not lagging in diligence, fervent in spirit, serving the Lord; rejoicing in hope, patient in tribulation, continuing steadfastly in prayer; distributing to the needs of the saints, given to hospitality" (Romans 12:11-13).

"not lagging in diligence" When you really love someone, you desire the best for them. So, in ministry, whatever you're doing, give it your best. Prepare well and pray well, then as you offer it, God will bless.

If Jesus were among us in bodily form, I think we would be falling all over ourselves asking, "Lord, what can I do for you? Can I get you something? Can I do this? Can I do that?" Friends, He is among you bodily, and He is saying, "In as much as you've done it to the least of my brothers and sisters, you do it to Me."

"fervent in spirit" Be *zealous*, aflame with the Spirit in serving the Lord Jesus Christ.

"rejoicing in hope" How do you endure tribulation while keeping a Christ-like attitude? To persevere, first you need to pray, then let the joy of your hope strengthen your heart. What is our hope? Jesus said, "Rejoice in this, that your name is written in heaven" (Luke 10:20). It's the hope of our salvation that lifts us.

"distributing to the needs of the saints" Proverbs 19:17 tells us, "He who is gracious to a poor man lends to the Lord, and He will repay him for his good deed." Our society says, "Invest in stocks that are really making money!" The Lord says, "Invest in people who cannot pay you back." The world says, "What a poor investment. You'll never see that again." But the Lord answers, "Yes, you will. I'm going to pay you back. It's a guarantee and the dividends are in heaven, and even on earth, I will bless you."

"given to hospitality" Hebrews 13:2 reminds us to "not forget to entertain strangers, for by so doing some have unwittingly entertained angels." Until you've opened your home to people who need a welcome, you'll never know what wonderful people, or even angels, you could be entertaining. At 99 years old, Abraham was sitting out in front of his house when three men walked by. He invited them to come share one of Sarah's scrumptious meals. These guys were angels... and the Lord Himself! Little did Abraham know that as the Lord stopped by that day, He would tell him, "And next year, that son I've been telling you about—he's yours." We need to carry on this tradition of hospitality by opening up our hearts and our lives.

Our Trademark Is Love

As Christians, love is our trademark. Many centuries ago, the heathen orator Aristedes, told the Emperor Hadrian what Christians are like: "They love one another. They never fail to help widows. They save orphans from those who would hurt them. If they have something, they give freely to those who have nothing. If they see a stranger, they take him home, and they're happy, as though he were a real brother. They don't consider themselves brothers in the usual sense that we think, but brothers instead through God." More and more, may this description of the first Christians be true of us today.

Chapter VIII
Showing The World God's Love

When my youngest son Nick was in kindergarten, I was driving him to school one day and I noticed he had his turtle puppet with him. So I asked him, "Hey Nick, why do you have your turtle with you?" He told me, "I'm taking him to show-and-tell." Now, Nick could have just told his fellow kindergartners about Mr. Turtle: "He's nice and soft and fluffy and green with a brown shell and button eyes...", but after a while, I'm sure all his classmates would have gotten bored. Instead, Nick brought the actual puppet, let them see it, touch it, and showed them how it worked. Seeing that puppet made much more of an impact than merely hearing about it.

While many Bible scriptures deal with *telling* the world the gospel, Romans 12:14-21 is about *showing* the world that God is real. If you only tell, but never show, you won't make much of an impact. The gospel itself has power within its own message, but if we live it, then as we speak, our words will "pack a wallop." By living out the goodness of God, nonbelievers can see what He is really like and they will be more apt to listen. People might not want to hear what we have to say, but if they see something radical in our lives, they'll sit up and take notice.

Let's examine what each of Paul's exhortations in Romans 12:14-21 can teach us about showing God's love to others.

Bless Your Persecutors

Verse 14: "Bless those who persecute you; bless and do not curse." I don't know about you, but my first reaction is to think, "Bless my persecutors? That's ridiculous! They're attacking me, and I'm supposed to bless them? I'd rather tell them off!" Our natural response is to curse, but we're not to respond naturally. If I respond in my human nature, how am I any different than non-Christians? As Jesus said, "If you love those who love you, what credit is that to you? For even sinners love those who love them" (Luke 6:32).

Jesus also said that God "makes His sun rise on the evil and on the good" (Matthew 5:45). What if every time we sinned, God said, "Okay, you're not going to see the sun for a week." God isn't like that. Even if we fail, God keeps giving His blessings, and extending His mercies and provisions. That's how He wants us to be towards others. Not discriminating if some people are mean, unlovely, or even mistreating us; not responding in the natural, but in the supernatural.

The devil and his demons are our real enemies. People who attack the cause of Christ are just pawns and captives in the devil's hands. How can we set them free? Certainly not by hating, lashing out, and cursing. First, we must pray that God will take the blindness off their eyes and break their bonds of slavery. But we really break down walls when we show them the love of Jesus. Bless them by doing some act of kindness, even though they treat you as an enemy.

The Greek word for "bless," is *eulogeao*, from which we get the word "eulogy," meaning "to speak well of." When we give a eulogy at a funeral, we are speaking well of the deceased. Those who curse Christians are spiritually dead. If we speak well of them and show them something good, perhaps the Lord can show Himself, raise them from the dead, and give them new life!

Rejoice And Weep

Verse 15: "Rejoice with those who rejoice, and weep with those who weep." Often, weeping with those who weep is much easier than rejoicing with those who rejoice, because sometimes, people are rejoicing over something we don't think they deserved—in fact, we may think we deserved that position or possession much more than they did, and they got it! Don't be jealous. The Lord wants to bless people, and there's plenty of blessings to go around. It may not be exactly what you had in mind, but He has something for you, so go ahead and rejoice with others. Praise the Lord that He is good. Be careful not to squelch people by pouring cold water on their joy.

To "weep with those who weep" means to have sympathy for others. I must confess, I've never liked sympathy and sentiment much. My father was quite sentimental, but he was an alcoholic and not very trustworthy. I got to the point where I would think, "Don't give me that sentimental business anymore." But over the years, I've seen so many people experience hurt and pain. Their lives have been wrecked by this fallen world, perhaps by their own sin, or by the hurtfulness of others. I've experienced grief myself, and those trials have tenderized me just like you tenderize meat with a fork. It has been good to be grieved, because pain has broken up my heart and helped me feel for others. Hebrews 4:15 says Jesus was "touched by the feeling of our infirmities." I pray that we too would have that heart for people.

Associate With The Humble

Verse 16: "Be of the same mind toward one another. Do not set your mind on high things, but associate with the humble. Do not be wise in your own opinion." There's a natural desire to gravitate towards beautiful, prominent, popular, and powerful people. We want to know them, because that somehow elevates us. Through my position as a pastor, I've been able to meet many Christian recording artists, professional athletes, and well-known speakers. Sometimes it can become a real "pride thing," but when that happens, I remind myself that God values all people. In fact, 1 Corinthians 12:23 says He gives more honor to the unseemly members of the body. Those are the ones we're walking right by in order to get to the seemly ones.

When we get a high opinion of ourselves or we're not associating with the humble, we miss out on the joy and the wonder of seeing Christ in action. How the Lord wants us to have humble hearts in this regard, and not think more highly of ourselves than we should—or think more highly of another, like they are some "pinnacle of success." We're servants, not stars. If you're looking for a stepping stone to be a star minister, or star musician, star this or that in the body of Christ, give it up and go back to being a servant. Then the Lord can lift you up.

Be A Peacemaker

Verses 17 and 18: "Repay no one evil for evil. Have regard for good things in the sight of all men. If it is possible, as much as depends on you, live peaceably with all men." From your side of any relationship, as much as you can, be a peacemaker. That's not always possible, which is why Paul says here, "as much as depends on you." Some people are going to be hostile towards you because of your love for Christ. Jesus said, "I didn't come to bring peace, but a sword, and the enemies of ones own household will be their own family members because of Me" (Matthew 10:34). Just make sure they are hostile because of Christ, not because you are being obnoxious or selfish, then saying "I'm persecuted for the Lord." We need to watch our hearts.

Love Your Enemies

Verses 19 and 20: "Beloved, do not avenge yourselves, but rather give place to wrath; for it

is written, 'Vengeance is Mine, I will repay,' says
the Lord. Therefore, 'If your enemy is hungry,
feed him; if he is thirsty, give him a drink. For in
so doing you will heap coals of fire on his
head.'" To repay evil for evil is to avenge
yourself, and vengeful people are the most sorry
people. They're negative, bitter, and warped.
The Bible tells us to be on our guards, lest a root
of bitterness grab hold of our heart and choke it
like a weed (Hebrews 12:15). James 1:20 says,
"The anger of men does not work the
righteousness of God." We might feel
righteously indignant, but that's not God's way.
Instead, He says, "When your enemy is hungry,
feed him. And when your enemy is thirsty, give
him a drink. For in so doing, you will heap coals
of fire upon his head."

We like this phrase because we think it
means, "Burn my enemy's head—allright!" But
let me tell you what it really means. There are
two possibilities: 1. In ancient times, they
actually did carry containers full of hot coals
upon their heads for their home fires.
Sometimes, they had to walk great distances to
get live, burning coals. So, to heap coals upon

someone's head would be to supply his need for home fuel. Or 2. By providing their need, you're heaping strong, burning conviction upon their mind. That is what will bring them to repentance. Romans 2:4 says the kindness of God melts us and brings us to repentance. Some people's consciences are so numb that it's going to take something shocking to revive them, and your loving them when they know they don't deserve it is going to blow their minds. This week, try bringing that belligerent boss of yours some cookies, or invite that nasty neighbor over for dinner. I'll tell you, it will change the whole composure of the relationship, and may even make them open to Christ.

Overcome Evil With Good

Verse 21: "Do not be overcome with evil, but overcome evil with good." This is a "double-barreled" command that every Christian should memorize. As you live in this evil world, you have one of two choices: To be overcome with evil, or to overcome evil with good. If you're not overcoming evil with the goodness of God in your life, you *will* be overcome by evil. The goodness of God is the key: We can't overcome evil in our own power, we must depend on the transforming power of Jesus Christ.

Living a life that seeks to help others find Christ will guard us from succumbing to evil. There's a true story that illustrates this truth: A man was lost in the wilderness during a terrible blizzard. After days of wandering around, he just couldn't take another step, so he fell into a snow bank. As the snow began to accumulate upon him, he knew he was going to die. But then, he felt movement beneath him and he began to dig under the snow. About a foot down, there was another man who was still alive. He thought, "I can't leave him here to die." So, motivated by the desire to save him, he mustered all his strength, put him on his shoulders, and began to plod forward again. Just fifty feet ahead, he found a cabin where they obtained shelter, food and fire wood. In saving the other man's life, his life was saved.

In the same way, our Christian lives are guarded from evil when we are on the offensive in our walks with the Lord. 1 Timothy 4:16 says that if we'll live to show others Christ's love, we will also guard our own salvation, thus protecting ourselves from being overcome by evil.

Empowered For Change

As I look at modern American society, I'm struck by the prevalence of evil. Everyday in so many ways, evil is "in your face," whether you like it or not. As Christians, it can seem overwhelmingly oppressive. We're concerned that our children will succumb, and we feel helpless to turn it around. But there is a way to make a difference: By taking every opportunity to apply these exhortations from Romans chapter 12, we can make a powerful impact in changing our world for Him and overcoming evil with good.

CHAPTER IX
GOOD CITIZENS / GOOD CHRISTIANS

During the week before His crucifixion,
Jesus had several confrontations with different
groups of people. On one occasion, the Pharisees
and the Herodians approached Jesus to try and
catch Him in a verbal blunder. They came on
real syrupy; trying to butter Jesus up so they
could eat Him alive. They gushed, "Oh Rabbi,
You are so true. You're the best teacher of God's
truth we've ever heard. You never just tell
people what they want to hear. You 'say it like it
is.' We like that. You're a great, great teacher. Is
it allright if we ask you just one little question?
Should we pay taxes to Caesar or not?" Jesus, of
course, could see right through their flattery. He
said to them, "Bring Me a tax coin and let Me see

it. Whose image and inscription is on this coin?"
"Caesar's," they answered. "Then render unto
Caesar what belongs to Caesar. And render unto
God what belongs to God." They were
dumbfounded. Jesus' statement was so
profound, people down to the present day still
quote the first half of this verse—every April 15
when taxes are due!

When Jesus said "render unto Caesar what
is Caesar's," He was telling us we are to be
subject to the governing authorities regarding
earthly matters. Romans 13:1-7 gives us three
reasons why we are to be subject to the
governing authorities: 1. For God's sake. 2. For
wrath's sake. 3. For conscience sake. As we look
at each of these, consider carefully how they
apply to you as a citizen of this world and as a
citizen of heaven.

Appointed By God

Verse 1: "Let every soul be subject to the
governing authorities. For there is no authority
except from God, and the authorities that exist
are appointed by God." Often it's hard to believe
that our governing authorities are appointed by

God, yet that's exactly what the Bible teaches. This doesn't mean that God is responsible for the sins of any government official, but it does mean that their authority to govern comes from Him.

There are no sinless politicians, nor are there perfect rulers, officials, or government authorities. The democrats aren't holy and the republicans aren't pure as the driven snow. Most politicians will claim to be on God's side at election time because it's an effective vote getting tool. But, regardless of who gets elected, whomever God ordains will still be a sinner while in office.

Whom Will God Choose?

God may not even give a country or a community the best or the godliest leader. In Daniel 4:17, Nebuchadnezzar, ruler over Babylon, acknowledges that he was set in that position by God, "In order that the living may know that the Most High rules in the kingdom of men and He gives it to whomever He wills and He sets over it the lowest of men." When he calls himself the "lowest," he is saying the

"basest" or the "most humiliating" among men.
Nebuchadnezzar thought he had made himself
the king of Babylon. He learned, the hard way,
that he didn't give himself that position of
power and prominence. God made him insane
for a while. He ended up going out in the fields
where he ate grass like a cow and his fingernails
grew into claws like a bird. Nebuchadnezzar
realized, "I guess I'm not as great as I thought I
was."

It was God who placed Nebuchadnezzar in
that position because He is the one who decides
who will rule over the kingdoms of men. Down
through the ages, God's people have wondered,
"Why would God appoint bad leaders?" The
Bible gives two answers. 1. God will give a
country what they deserve. He gives people the
level of leaders who fit the overall moral and
spiritual character of the nation; who fit the
spiritual quality of the populace. 2. God ordains
immoral leaders sometimes in order to prepare a
nation for either repentance or judgment. If a
nation has an oppressive leader, it might come
to the point of crying out to God for help. With
that seeking of God, there can be revival and

reformation. If repentance doesn't happen, God grants us immoral leaders so that when He judges us, He will be blameless in doing so.

I believe these are the reasons why America is plagued with leaders and judges who have made immoral decisions and judgments. They have brought us to the brink of desperately needing large-scale repentance. We need spiritual and moral revival so badly. If that doesn't happen, He will bring large scale judgment upon our nation. Really, our own sins are judging us, because you cannot sin without the consequences of disease, pain and suffering. Even physical disasters could be the beginning of God shaking us and saying, "Hey, wake up!"

Is there anything we can do? "If my people who are called by My name will humble themselves and pray and seek my face, then I will hear from heaven and I will forgive their sins and heal their land" (2 Chronicles 7:14). We need to be seeking God, calling upon Him to heal our land.

Submit To Authority

Since the governing authorities are ordained by God, we as Christians should submit to them. We, of all people, should respect authority and be good, law-abiding citizens. In words similar to Jesus', Paul tells us how to conduct ourselves in verse 7 "Render therefore to all their due; taxes to whom taxes are due, customs to whom customs, fear to whom fear, honor to whom honor." Peter makes a similar statement: "Having your conduct honorable among the Gentiles, that when they speak against you as evildoers, they may, by your good works which they observe, glorify God in the day of visitation. Therefore, submit yourselves to every ordinance of man for the Lord's sake, whether to the king as supreme, or to governors, as to those who are sent by Him for the punishment of evildoers and for the praise of those who do good. For this is the will of God, that by doing good you may put to silence the ignorance of foolish men—as free, yet not using liberty as a cloak for vice, but as bondservants of God. Honor all people. Love the brotherhood. Fear God. Honor the king" (1 Peter 2:12-17).

These verses proclaim a New Testament truth: We are to be submissive to the government. We're to be good citizens, not rebels. In Paul and Peter's day, Jewish zealots were using violence to further their agenda. But the apostles are drawing a line here, saying, "Believers in Christ, don't do that." Believers in Christ have a different way of conquering their world: Changing lives by sharing the love of God and the good news of Jesus Christ—that's our calling.

Paul and Peter both insist, "Honor the king." Do you know which king they were saying to honor? Nero, one of the most despicable, wicked, yucky guys who has ever lived! They weren't honoring Nero for his person, but for his position. We need to be careful to respect and honor our leaders for the position God has given them. That doesn't mean we must agree with their politics or even appreciate their character. But we should still show respect, not dishonor. More importantly, we need to pray for our officials. If we would pray more and criticize less, oh what the Lord could do! That's why Paul told Timothy to pray and intercede for all people, especially all who are in authority (1 Timothy 2:1,2). Prayer will create a spiritual climate where the gospel and the people of God can flourish.

Pray And Pay

We are both to pray and to pay "taxes to whom taxes are due" (verse 7). Let's face it, taxation is the one thing our government does well! Verse 6 says the government authorities "attend continually to this very thing"—they do attend to taxing us *continually!* Allow me to share a few tax quips: "When filling out your income tax report, be sure not to overlook your biggest dependent, the government." "Patrick Henry ought to come back and see what taxation *with* representation is like." Will Rogers said, "Just be glad you're not getting all the government you paid for."

Though we joke about the IRS, we as Christians are to pay all of our taxes. We shouldn't cheat or justify not paying Uncle Sam his due. I met a fellow once who believed Christians didn't need to pay taxes because, he said, "It's unconstitutional." I told him "You're not just in rebellion against the IRS and the civil authorities, you're in severe rebellion against God. God has ordained the authorities and He wants us to submit, because in doing so, we're submitting to Him."

God's Ministers

For what purposes has God appointed government authorities? Verse 4: "For he is God's minister to you for good. But if you do evil, be afraid; for he does not bear the sword in vain; for he is God's minister, an avenger to execute wrath on him who practices evil." Paul calls these authorities "God's ministers." The word "minister" is "deacon," meaning "practically serving the needs of the people for God." There are two ways that all governments have a deacon ministry to its people—one is positive, the other negative, but they are both for our good.

God's Ministers For Our Benefit

The positive reason: "he is God's minister to you for good" or "for your benefit," to perform certain services and give certain benefits where appropriate. A good example is our water supply. It would be difficult for each of us to have our own, private water supply. Other examples are our sewage system, our power supply, and roadway management. What if we each had to build our own highways? The government has an obligation to provide these services.

The government should also provide even beyond such things for those who are truly disabled and for valid reasons they or their family cannot meet their needs. Some people say, "The government has no place in that kind of ministry." It does. The government is to be God's minister to us for good, but it's not to do for people what they are able and should do for themselves.

Someone has said, "A government big enough to give people all they want is also big enough to take from people all they've got." People need to trust in God first, then themselves, and not so much in the government. The government is not our savior. We need to look to God and let Him show us how to take care of ourselves. That's not to say that the government doesn't play a positive role in providing benefits. This is where the debate is: To what degree should the government provide? Within the framework of this debate, there is room for differing opinions among Christians. Since we live in a democracy, we as voters have opportunities to make sure the government doesn't overstep its bounds, nor understep its responsibilities.

God's Ministers For Our Protection

The second God appointed ministry of the government is the negative one: Protecting the people from criminals, from evil, and from harm: Verse 4: "if you do evil, be afraid; for he does not bear the sword in vain; for he is God's minister, an avenger to execute wrath on him who practices evil." The authorities are God's ministers to avenge domestic criminals and foreign adversaries in order to protect its people. The government has a responsibility to see to it that the police protect law abiding citizens from criminals and punish law breakers. If they're not punishing the lawless while giving the citizens a sense of security, the government is failing. When a criminal's rights become more attended to than the victim's rights, the government is failing. That's where we've come in our country. Within the American judicial system, criminals are not receiving firm, swift judgment and punishment. As a result, there is so much fear, you can hardly walk out on the streets.

Capital Punishment

To what degree has God delegated authority and appointed the civil government to execute judgment? According to verse 4, to the extent of executing capital punishment on those who deserve it: "If you do evil, be afraid; for he [the authority that God has ordained] does not bear the sword in vain." The word "sword" only had one meaning in the Roman empire: death. It meant execution. Yes, God has ordained capital punishment to deter crime and has delegated that authority to earthly leaders.

In Genesis 9:6, God gave Noah a law for punishing crime in the post-flood era that still applies today: "Whoever sheds man's blood, by man his blood shall be shed. For in the image of

God He made man." Some will say, "Only God has the right to take a life." That's true, but God has invested in the civil authorities to act in His place and execute His judgment when a crime is committed deserving of death.

You might be thinking, "That doesn't sound very compassionate or Christ-like." It is Christ-like. Jesus believed in judgment and in justice, and we must as well. You say, "But Christ also believed in mercy." Many people don't see their need for mercy until they receive justice. If you keep showing mercy to someone who has no respect for justice whatsoever, they will continue in sin and immorality. How many people must be hurt before they see their need for mercy? To show mercy to capital offenders, we should put them on death row, then send in gospel workers to share the love of Christ. Hopefully, they will repent, receive Christ, and be eternally changed on the inside, then let them die for what they did. If they did repent and trust Christ, they'll immediately go to heaven.

Others will say, "Capital punishment does not deter crime." Oh yes it does—when you're dead, you do not commit another crime. Our system should execute firm and swift judgment after a fair and just trial. These endless appeals where for years people are not punished for the heinous crimes they have committed don't deter anyone, they just encourage the rampant crime we see today. There are those who have different viewpoints than what I am stating, and I respect that. But in no way can you prove that capital punishment is unbiblical.

For Wrath And Conscience Sake

For wrath's sake and for conscience sake, we must be submissive to the governing authorities. Verse 3: "For rulers are not a terror to good works, but to evil. Do you want to be unafraid of the authority? Do what is good, and you will have praise from the same." Because we fear wrath, we want to do what is right. We don't want to be punished and judged because we've broken the law. I don't know about you, but when I'm driving down the street and I see a policeman, my first i inclination is to be afraid! My second inclination is to look at the speedometer and simultaneously step on the brake, whether I need to or not—it's total instinct! Why am I afraid? Because in the past I've been stopped, I've been punished, I've had to pay, and I don't like it! I'm a law-breaker in that way, but I'm being reformed. But you know what's interesting? If I see that I'm going the speed limit, I'm not afraid at all! I look at that policeman, wave and say, "Hi officer! Good to see you!" The authorities will praise you and your witness will be good if you're a law abiding citizen.

Regarding our conscience, we shouldn't just keep the law only because we're afraid of being punished, but because we want to please God. We want a strong faith and fellowship with God, but if we have a guilty conscience, we won't have a strong faith. 1 John 3:4 says the essence of sin is lawlessness. Lawlessness says, "I'm not going to submit to your authority. I'll do whatever I please. No one tells me what to do." Pleasing God says, "God, I will submit to You."

Civil Disobedience

Is there a place, because of conscience, for civil disobedience? When the government commands you to do something that God has said you cannot do, not just taking your tax money and doing it themselves, then it is time for peaceful civil disobedience. When Peter and John were told not to share the gospel, Peter said, "What you do, we cannot say. You must do what you think is right. But as for us, we must obey God rather than man." Our ultimate authority is God. We cannot do what God has said not to do. Peter and Paul loved the Lord so much, they wouldn't quit telling the world about the risen Jesus Christ. The Roman authorities demanded, "Quit speaking that name! You quit saying 'Christ is Lord.' Say 'Caesar is Lord.'" They looked them square in the face and said, "Christ is Lord." For their absolute devotion to Christ, Paul's head was chopped off and Peter was crucified upside-down.

Thankfully, our country hasn't gotten to that point yet. We should be thankful that our government hasn't deteriorated that much, but it could. Regardless, "Render to God what belongs to God," because His image and inscription are stamped upon you. Give to Him your life, follow Him, pledge your life to Him, and in doing that, be a good citizen.

CHAPTER X

PAYING OUR LOVE DEBT

In Romans 13:8, we find a great command: "Owe no one anything except to love one another." Each and every Christian owes a huge debt of love that is to be paid back by loving others. On the cross, Jesus paid in full the massive debt the world had chalked up: that moral debt of sin against God. Why did Jesus pay this debt? Love. "For God exhibits Christ's love toward us in that while we were yet sinners, Jesus Christ died in our place" (Romans 5:8). Christ pouring out His blood and hanging on the cross was the ultimate exhibition of love.

Infinite love paid the debt for our sins, so we owe a debt of infinite love to Jesus. There's no way we could ever pay it off—it's too big! Don't you hate to have debts you can't pay?

But in this case, don't be discouraged because that's the Lord's plan. He *knows you* owe a debt you can never pay, and He wants you to make small installments everyday, forever! Each and every single day, give others some of His love. In so doing, you're actually making payments to Jesus for the love He has given to us. Jesus said, "In as much as you show love to others, you are doing it as unto Me" (Matthew 25:40). When you visit those who are alone, when you feed the hungry, when you take care of the sick, when you provide for the needy, Jesus says, "You're doing it unto Me—you're paying Me back."

Pay Jesus Back With Love

If you owe someone money, it's uncomfortable to be around them. The whole time, you're wondering if they're thinking about that debt. I remember one time, I owed my brother a few hundred dollars. I love my brother, but during that period, I didn't want to see him. When we had family gatherings, I would stand on the other side of the room. I avoided him, or if we did communicate, I would make it quick. It was such a relief when I was finally able to pay him back—a burden was lifted.

In the same way, we are to sense our obligation to love others because of our debt to Jesus. When we meet people, seeing them should remind us that Christ died for them. We owe it to them to give out a little bit of His love. When you pay that debt by loving those He brings across your path, it makes you joyful and you feel relief. When you're impatient, unkind, and so caught up in yourself that you're unloving, you go away feeling like you've cheated the Lord. He gave you a chance to make a payment and you missed it.

A Log Jam In Your Heart

You might say, "I just don't have that kind of love," but you are able to make those love payments if you have the Holy Spirit. Romans 5:5 says the love of God is poured out in our hearts by the Holy Spirit who was given to us. Jesus said the Holy Spirit is like a river, pouring forth into and through our lives. If He is not, maybe something is blocking the flow. Every once in a while, I'll have a log jam in my heart. I just don't feel like being around people. I'll see an opportunity to witness and say, "Forget it, Lord. I'm not in the mood." When a log jam happens, I pray about it and have others pray for me that God will remove the barrier, so His love can flow. When the dam breaks, once again I'm able to love as He loves in the power of His Spirit.

Love Is The Fulfillment Of The Law

An expert in the Mosaic Law came to Jesus and asked, "'Teacher, which is the first commandment of all?' Jesus answered him, 'The first of all the commandments is: 'Hear, O Israel, the Lord our God, the Lord is one. And you shall love the Lord your God with all your heart [all your feelings and will], with all your soul [your entire personality], and with all your mind [all your thoughts], and with all your strength [all your energy].' This is the first commandment. And the second, like it, is this: 'You shall love your neighbor as yourself. There

is no other commandment greater than these"'
(Mark 12:28-31).

God's entire commandment system hangs
on love. Twice, in Romans 13:8 and 10, Paul says
"love is the fulfillment of the law." The word
"fulfill" means to "cram full to overflowing," or
"completely fulfill the law." In other words, love
does above and beyond what the law requires.
We see this in verse 9 where five "shall not"
commands are given: "For the commandments,
'You shall not commit adultery,' 'You shall not
murder,' 'You shall not steal,' 'You shall not bear
false witness,' "You shall not covet,' and if there
is any other commandment, are all summed up
in this saying, namely, 'You shall love your
neighbor as yourself.' Love does no harm to a
neighbor; therefore love is the fulfillment of the
law."

These are commands that God has given to
protect us from harming one another. For
example, it says, "You shall not commit
adultery." If I love you, I'm not going to want to
be sexually involved with your mate. "You shall
not murder." If I love you, I'm not going to shoot

you. "You shall not steal." If I love you, I won't take what is not mine. "You shall not bear false witness." If I love you, I won't lie to you. "You shall not covet." If I love you, I will rejoice in what you have, not want it for myself.

Love Your Neighbor As Yourself

We can see that love won't break these commands, but in fact, love is much more than this—love is more than not doing harm. Love is doing positive acts that help others. It's taking their needs upon yourself and making them your own. To "love your neighbor as yourself" means seeing someone else's needs and wanting to meet them. That's love.

Often when I'm sharing Christ with someone, they say to me, "Well, I'm a good person. I never hurt anyone." The fact that you never hurt anyone doesn't prove you're a good person. It just proves you're not a criminal. That's wonderful—it's great that you don't commit grand larceny, or murder, or lie and cheat, or assault people. But that doesn't make you a good person. The Bible says no one is good in comparison to Jesus Christ. When it comes to loving our neighbor as ourselves, we all fall short. And even when we look at the those five commands in verse 8, I think we must come to the conclusion that we do hurt others:

"Thou shalt not commit adultery" So many people today are sexually involved with someone to whom they're not legally married. This has become an accepted practice in our society. People will justify it by saying, "We're in love." But this verse is saying "love does not commit adultery." If you are sexually involved with someone out of wedlock, you're not in love, you're in sin. This is not a demonstration of love. Instead, it's showing that you don't care about their highest well being, because if you did, you would care about their relationship with God.

If this is a problem you are having right now, I believe God is saying to you, "I want to change you. I want to show you what real love is. I want you to repent. Quit sinning." Ask God's forgiveness, let Him cleanse you, and let Him help you give that person the love and respect they deserve. Then you can really love them in the way God wants you to love.

"Thou shalt not commit murder" We murder people's reputations with our sharp, "forked tongues," don't we? 1 John 3:14,15 says, "He who does not love his brother abides in spiritual death. Whoever hates his brother is a murderer." To be unloving is spiritual death.

"Thou shalt not steal" We can steal by not giving an honest, full day's work. Have you ever done that? As a pastor, my boss is the Lord and I'm accountable to Him. But I must confess, there have been days when I haven't put my entire energy into my work. I'm stealing, and the Lord speaks to me about it. I'm glad He does.

"Thou shalt not bear false witness" Beware of half truths that deceive, and beware of portraying an image that isn't reality. This is a problem in our society which loves to promote its motto: "Image is everything."

"Thou shalt not covet" You can gauge your "coveting level" when your neighbor drives up in a new car—the very model and color you've been wanting. Are you able to "rejoice with him who rejoiceth," or do you look at that new car

and sigh, "Oh, that's nice." What if your friend
gets a new outfit that you know would look
great on you? Are you happy for them? Or
inside, are you really bummed out, wondering,
"Why don't I have the stuff they have?" as your
"covet-meter" goes off the scale?

Let Jesus Replace You

When I see these commands in this way, I
look at myself and say, "Wow, Lord, I have
fallen short. I am guilty." But Jesus can make me
a loving person by replacing myself with
Himself. I'm not loving because I'm filled with
me, myself, and I—three guys who always get in
the way! But if I let Christ take care of me,
myself, and I, then I can take care of others. So
often, we fight for our way because we don't
think the Lord will take care of us. Without
saying it, we grumble, "You're not doing a good
job of taking care of me, Lord. Come on!"

Jesus will take care of you. Maybe you're not
allowing Him to provide. Or perhaps you're not
close enough to Him to sense the fulfillment He
offers. All I know is that God said He would
supply *all* our needs "according to His riches in

Christ Jesus" (Philippians 4:19). Put yourself in His hands and say, "Lord, You take care of me. I know you're good. I want to give to others what You've given me in abundance."

You've probably heard this before, but the key to joy is: **J**esus first, **O**thers second, **Y**ourself third—that's **JOY**. Many of us are filled with **YOJ** or **OYJ**. When you're putting yourself first, or even when you're putting others ahead of Jesus, there's disorder, and you can't give in the way He wants you to give.

Love One Another

Whom are we to love? Verse 8 tell us to "love one another." First of all, we are to love our Christian brothers and sisters—the family of God. Paul told the Galatians, "Therefore, as we have opportunity, let us do good to all, especially to those who are of the household of faith" (Galatians 6:10). So you say, "That's great. No problem. I'll be glad to love God's people." But *three times* in Romans 13, Paul tells us to love our neighbor: At the end of verse 9: "love your neighbor as yourself;" verse 8: "He who loves another has fulfilled the law;" and verse 10:

"Love does no harm to a neighbor; therefore love is the fulfillment of the law." Some people might respond, "I live out in the country, so I don't have any neighbors to love. Praise the Lord!" But loving our neighbor means much more than just being nice to the guy next door.

Who is our neighbor?

Jesus had an exchange with an expert in religion who asked, "Lord, what can I do to inherit eternal life?" Jesus said, "What does the Scripture say to you?" The expert answered, "Love God with all your heart, soul, strength, and mind, and love your neighbor as yourself." Jesus responded, "That's a good answer. Do it and you will live." Then the expert asked, "Who is my neighbor?"

Jesus answered with the story of the Good Samaritan: There was a man who went on a journey from Jerusalem down to Jericho. This was a dangerous road, because there were many shadowy spots; it was very hilly with lots of places for robbers to hide. Sure enough, this man was walking along when some thieves jumped out of the shadows and beat him, threw him on the ground and stripped him, took everything he had and left him there half dead. A priest came walking by and saw him lying there, then crossed over to the other side, perhaps thinking, "If I don't get too close, I can't be held responsible." Then a Levite came along. He also crossed over to the other side, pretending not to see, because "Ignorance is bliss." Then a Samaritan came by and immediately went to the man. When he saw him hurt, he felt great compassion. He brought out his first-aid kit, took the oil and the wine and washed his wounds, then bandaged him up. Then he put him on his horse and dropped him off at the hospital saying, "This guy has been hurt. Take care of him and Ill come back in a few days to pay the bill."

Jesus said to the religious expert, "Which one of them was a neighbor to this man?" It was obvious, so of course he answered, "The one who showed him mercy was the real neighbor." Jesus said, "That's right. Go and do the same."

Jesus, the Good Samaritan

Jesus is our Good Samaritan. Jesus saw you hurt. He saw that the world had done some damage to your life, that your sin and the sin of others had robbed you, and He felt compassion. He couldn't just pass you by. Jesus went right to you and took the wine of His blood and began to wash those wounds and apply the oil of His Spirit. He comforted and ministered to you, then He took you to His hospital—the body of Christ—and said, "Bless this one for Me, and I'll pay the bill."

What a bill we keep running up, but the Lord is more than willing to take care of us. Jesus is saying, "You have an infinite debt of love to repay and there are so many others who need My help. Take what I give you and give it to them. Pay Me back, a little bit each day, for the love I've given to you."

CHAPTER XI
RISE AND SHINE

I'm sure if we were to take a poll of everyone's favorite household appliance, one that would not win would be the alarm clock. I tend to hate my alarm clock because it wakes me up out of sleep, and I love to sleep. I used to have an alarm clock that would go off every morning with a loud, obnoxious blast—it sounded like an air raid siren! I got rid of that clock and got one that chirped. It was very pleasant, but those little bird noises didn't always wake me up. Now, I've got an alarm clock that sounds like a telephone busy signal and (this is my favorite part), it has one of those "snooze" buttons. Sometimes I'll hit that button eight times before I get up! Proverbs 27:14 says,

"He who blesses his friend with a loud voice early in the morning, it will be reckoned a curse to him." That describes an alarm clock. You feel like cursing it, yet it is your friend because it gets you up.

In Romans 13:11-14, Paul is sounding our wake up call: "And do this, knowing the time, that now it is high time to awake out of sleep; for now our salvation is nearer than when we first believed. The night is far spent, the day is at hand. Therefore let us cast off the works of darkness, and let us put on the armor of light. Let us walk properly, as in the day, not in revelry and drunkenness, not in lewdness and lust, not in strife and envy. But put on the Lord Jesus Christ, and make no provision for the flesh, to fulfill its lusts." Paul is saying, "It's late! Christ is coming soon! It's high time we wake up out of our spiritual laziness and lethargy. Open those sleepy eyes of faith and behold Jesus, your lovely Lord. Rise up and let the light of Christ shine through you. Stop sleep-walking in sin, rouse yourself, get clothed with Christ, and get going for the Lord!"

Christ's Appearing

Do you realize that the time is short? It's late in God's prophetic time table for this world. When Paul wrote these words in 58 AD, he said "the night is far spent, the day [of the Lord] is at hand" (verse 12). If that was true in 58 AD, how much truer it is today. To use Paul's illustration of a 24 hour day, if there were just a couple of hours left until the dawning of Christ's appearing when Paul wrote this, we must be down to a couple of minutes, or even a few seconds until the day of Christ will be here!

God wants His people to live in the consciousness that Jesus is coming soon. He doesn't want us to think, "Well, Paul said He was coming soon back then and He didn't, so I guess He's not coming soon now, either." Rather, living with a sense of expectancy helps us to treasure eternal life more than this temporal life. Jesus said, "Don't lay up for yourself treasures on earth where moth and rust destroy, and thieves break in and steal, but lay up for yourself treasures in heaven where moth and rust can't destroy, and thieves cannot come in and steal. For where your treasure is, there will your heart be also" (Matthew 6:19-21). Jesus didn't say, "Where your heart is, there will your treasure be." No, where your treasure is, there your heart will follow.

Treasure Jesus

Recently, I was going through a very weary period, almost coming to the point of numbness. I had been incredibly busy, and a close loved one had just passed away after a two year battle with cancer. Frankly, I was "burned out." I wanted to be honest before the Lord about these negative attitudes, so I made a list titled, "Things I Don't Care About." Here's what I listed: 1. Ministry. 2. Prayer. 3. People. Isn't that terrible? You don't get very far as a pastor if you don't like people, prayer, or ministry! But that was my state of mind. Deep down, I still had a heart of love for the Lord, but all I could feel was this ambivalence towards the ministry He had given me. I'm not used to feeling that way, so I told the Lord, "I don't want to be like this." A few days later, I woke up in the middle of the night with this Scripture on my mind, "Where your treasure is, there will your heart be." Then it hit me: I'd been treasuring the ministry, people, and religious activity, but I hadn't been treasuring Christ. He was telling me, "I want you to treasure Me, just enjoy Me."

Even good things can burn us out. When we're worn out, what we need most is Jesus. He wants us to set our hearts on Him, but we won't if we're laying up for ourselves treasures upon the earth as the main thrust of our lives. When Jesus Christ comes, will He find us building His kingdom, or will He find us building our own? We are to lay up treasures for the eternal life we're going to have, not waste all our energy on things that are going to perish.

Take Every Opportunity

We can be absolutely sure that we are nearer to seeing Jesus face to face than we've ever been before. Even if He doesn't come in our lifetime, not too many years from now, we will go to be with Him. In fact, within 50 years or so, many or most of us are going to be gone.

What can we do to make sure that when we stand before the Lord, our lives will have counted for eternity? In verse 11, Paul says, "And do this, knowing the time" referring back to verse 9 where he told us to "Love your neighbor as yourself." We are to live a life of love: loving God, receiving God's love, and paying our debt back to Him by loving others. The time to love people is diminishing. The opportunities you had yesterday are gone, but you have more opportunities today. Paul told the Ephesians to "buy up every opportunity." Don't pass up the chances He gives you to love people for Him.

Clothed In Christ

Verses 12-14 give us some guidelines on how we should live: "Therefore let us cast off the works of darkness, and let us put on the armor of light. Let us walk properly, as in the day, not in revelry and drunkenness, not in lewdness and lust, not in strife and envy. But put on the Lord Jesus Christ, and make no provision for the flesh, to fulfill its lusts."

The picture Paul is painting is that of throwing off filthy, gross clothes, and instead putting on clean, graceful garments. I remember one time I was asked to speak at my children's school convocation. That particular day I was out working somewhere and I'd lost track of the time. I had old, dirty clothes on, but if I'd gone home to change, I would have been late, so I decided to drive straight to the school. When I got there, I found that everyone was dressed to the hilt! As I came in the back door, people kept looking at me, probably wondering, "Who's that guy? The janitor?" I recognized my friend, Tom, standing near the back with a nice suit and tie on. After I called Tom over and told him the situation, we went in the bathroom where I took off my grubby clothes and Tom gave me his suit. I put it on, looked great, and was able to give my speech. We even found some spare clothes for Tom to wear (no, he didn't have to hide in the bathroom!)

It would have been disgraceful for me to address that gathering in dirty clothes. In the same way, verse 12 says, "Let us cast off the works of darkness." Paul is saying, "Throw away those dirty, filthy ways of living and put on the pure and holy garments of salvation. Get rid of the things that are indecent and unfitting for a child of God. They are embarrassing and dishonoring to the Lord." In verse 13, Paul tells us what those "works of darkness" are:

Revelry - loose, sensual partying and carousing. This doesn't mean Christians can't have fun and enjoy exuberant times, of course we can, but not if the atmosphere is sensual and loose.

Drunkenness - drinking to feel good and get high. Ephesians 5:18 says, "Don't be drunk with wine, but rather be filled with God's Spirit." Be excited about the Lord, let Him fill you and make you feel good.

Lewdness - shameful, gross talk and behavior. We live in a lewd generation in America, thanks largely to the media and entertainment industry. Acts that before were done in secret are now out there for everyone to wallow in. We're not to be a part of that.

Lust or licentiousness - sexual passion out of the bounds of marriage.

Strife - selfish ambition; stepping on people to get ahead; fighting to be number one instead of letting God raise you up.

Envy - being jealous or covetous in any way.

Wake Up!

Throw off the works of darkness. As Christians, we're to be people of light. I love what Paul told the Ephesians, "For you were once darkness, but now you are light in the Lord. Walk as children of light (for the fruit of the Spirit is in all goodness, righteousness, and truth), finding out what is acceptable to the Lord. And have no fellowship with the unfruitful works of darkness, but rather, expose them. For it is shameful even to speak of those things which are done by them in secret. But all things that are exposed are made manifest by the light, for whatever makes manifest is light. Therefore He says: 'Awake, you who sleep, Arise from the dead, And Christ will give you light'" (Ephesians 5:8-14). Again, Paul is saying,

"Wake up!" Arise and let Christ shine on you and shine *through you.*

When you were in school, did you ever fall asleep in class? Maybe you didn't get much sleep the night before, or perhaps the teacher's boring, so you put your head down on your book "just for a second." Before you know it, you're dreaming! Then, something startles you and you jerk your head up, hoping no one saw you sleeping or noticed the drool spot on your notebook! Or even worse, you wake up because you hear your name called. The teacher is asking you a question, but you can't answer because you were asleep.

You know, it's the same way spiritually. When you get lazy spiritually, when you are not paying attention to the Lord, when He becomes a low priority, you become dull. People come along who need answers, but you can't really show them Christ because you're not spiritually alert. You don't even want to talk to anyone about the Lord. That's sad, but it doesn't need to be that way. Instead, "put on the armor of light" (verse 12). Wake up, pray, seek the Lord.

Jesus took Peter, James, and John, to the Garden of Gethsemane because He needed some friends to pray with Him. But each time He came back, they were sleeping. This was the darkest time in their lives, and they were sleeping! The Lord asked them, "Could you not watch with Me one hour? Watch and pray, lest you enter into temptation. The spirit is willing, but the flesh is weak" (Matthew 26:40,41). If you're having hard times and the battle is fierce spiritually, it's not the time to be sleeping. Yes, get enough sleep physically, but also make sure that you're taking time to wait on the Lord. "The spirit is willing, but the flesh is weak," so you must feed and fuel the spirit.

Dispel The Darkness

How is darkness dispelled? Not by beating it out or shooing it away with our own effort. When you come into a dark room, you don't yell, "Darkness, get out of here! Shoo!" No, you just turn on the light switch. As Christians, we sometimes think, "I've got to grit my teeth and get this sin out of my life!" Turn on the light of Christ. "In Him was life, and the life was the light of men. And the light shines in the darkness, and the darkness did not overcome it" (John 1:4,5).

How do you walk in the light everyday? There are four ways: 1. Prayer. "For You will light my lamp; the Lord my God will enlighten my darkness" (Psalm 18:28). 2. The Bible. "Thy Word is a lamp unto my feet and a light unto my path" (Psalm 119:105). Don't just depend on Sundays. Read a portion of His Word every single day. 3. His presence. "God is light, and in Him there is no darkness at all. If we say that we have fellowship with God and yet walk in darkness we are lying, but if we walk in the light with Him, we have fellowship with one another and the blood of Jesus will cleanse our lives from sin" (1 John 1:5-7). Draw close to God because His presence is light. 4. Receive His love and walk in His love. "He who loves His brother lives in God's light and there is no cause for stumbling in him" (1 John 2:10).

Make No Provision

Verse 14 contains the "bottom line": "Put on the Lord Jesus Christ, and make no provision for the flesh, to fulfill its lusts." Paul doesn't say, "Make a little provision for fleshly, sinful desires." Don't say this to yourself, "I've been a good Christian lately, so I'll go ahead and sin, I've earned it." Living this way only squelches your joy and your reward. Put on Jesus and "make *no* provision for the flesh."

To "make provision" means to "take forethought," or giving temptation place in your mind, secretly expecting to gratify it at a later more opportune time. It's letting temptation come along, then thinking, "This is not the right time or place. Too many people around. I'll file it, and later, 'we shall enter in.'" Don't let those thoughts have lodging in your mind. Just say "No!" Make *no* provision for the flesh, but rather, put on the Lord Jesus Christ. Clothe yourself with Him.

When I was a kid, I had a reoccurring dream in which I went outside naked. In those nightmares, I would keep trying to cover myself up because I was so embarrassed. When I would finally wake up, I was *so* glad I was dreaming! That's why you get dressed in the morning before you leave the house—you don't want to make a fool out of yourself. And you wear clothes all day long. You don't go through half the day then say, "I think I'll take my clothes off now." You put on the appropriate clothes for covering, so you'll be presentable, or maybe even to make a good impression at an important appointment.

Jesus is telling us, "Put Me on first thing in the morning, then all day long let Me be your best attire because My goodness makes such a great impression. My love makes a wonderful presentation and My holiness is so appropriate. The flesh is embarrassing. It's shameful. Don't let people see you like that!" Do you see how important it is to get close to God first thing everyday? Even if you only have a few minutes, draw close to Him and say, "Lord, cover me today. Fill me today."

CHAPTER XII

THE ABUNDANT CHRISTIAN LIFE

"Now may the God of hope fill you with all joy and peace in believing, that you may abound in hope by the power of the Holy Spirit" (Romans 15:13). In this prayer, Paul expresses the pinnacle of God's desire for your life. The Lord doesn't want to put a frown on your face by burdening you with religious restrictions. Jesus came "that you might have life and that you might have it abundantly" (John 10:10). His desire is for you to have an abundance of His joy and peace filling your life, spiritually and emotionally abounding in hope.

Why is this God's will? First of all, because He loves us and wants to bless us. Jesus observed, "If you being evil know how to give good things to your children, how much more your heavenly Father (who is not evil) will give good gifts to those who ask Him?" (Matthew 7:11). Secondly, when God fills our lives with hope, joy, and peace, the overflow of His blessings ministers to others and they will want to receive from the Lord as well.

Sample His Goodness

Let me illustrate: My family loves to go to the supermarket when they're giving out free samples. They might have a new chip and dip, or maybe they're promoting a cracker or cookie, sometimes they even have electric frying pans cooking up little sausages— Yummy! I love eating those free samples. I remember once visiting an exhibit at the Washington State Fair where they had free samples of lentil soup. We hadn't eaten lunch, so we had about 20 little cups full. But do you know what those free samples did to us more than anything else? They made us want to buy that delicious soup. Their spacious booth hadn't attracted us, nor did the big "Lentil Soup" sign. But when we smelled the soup cooking and saw that it was free, that drew us over. Then tasting clinched the sale... they made a killing off of us that day!

The Lord wants to use you and I as free samples, drawing people so they can "taste and see that the Lord is good" (Psalm 34:8). It's great to talk about how good the Lord is, but we also need to show His goodness. Grant someone mercy, "cut them some slack," give a "random act of kindness" out of the abundance He has given you. God's goodness in our lives is the juicy bait on His hook that catches people. Once they taste, if they know that it's really Him, then they're hooked.

Filled Up With Jesus

In order for us to offer samples of the Lord to others, we must learn how we can experience more and more of what Paul prays for us in Romans 15:13, "Now may the God of hope fill you with all joy and peace in believing, that you may abound in hope by the power of the Holy Spirit." This is the only verse in the Bible where God is called "the God of hope." This beautiful title is used in conjunction with how He wants to fill our lives. He is the God of hope, not just for some general, nebulous reason, but for the specific purpose of filling us with joy and peace in believing, that we may abound in hope ourselves.

Perhaps you haven't experienced an abundance of joy and hope in your Christian life, or you've come to the point of giving up on the idea of having abundant life in Jesus. Maybe you're thinking, "Yeah, Jesus said He can give us abundant life, but that's for the super-spiritual people. They can have that, but not me." Don't give up and settle for something less than God's highest will. God has an ideal for your life, and He will bring you along to where you can receive what He has for you.

A Vision Of Hope

The abundant fruit of the Spirit takes time and must be cultivated to grow. Yes, we can be filled with the Spirit at certain points in time, but cultivating joy and hope is an ongoing process. Even the best gardeners don't produce flowers and fruit-bearing trees overnight. When we first moved into our house, the yard looked like a vacant lot. But my wife Cathy had a "vision of hope" for the land. Now, I didn't have this vision. In fact, Cathy didn't share her ideas with me for a year or two. Then one day, she laid before me a blueprint of our yard with every square inch planned out. I couldn't visualize it... for me, it didn't seem like hope, it just looked like work! But Cathy had that vision of hope, and then through a labor of love, our yard was transformed into a lovely English garden.

God has a plan of hope for you. Others may not see any potential, or have much hope that you'll amount to anything for the Lord. Who cares what they think. You need to zero in on God and the plan of hope He has for you. Jeremiah 29:11 says, "'For I know the plans I have for you,' declares the Lord. 'Plans for well-being and not for evil, to give you a future and a hope.'" That's why you should never settle for less than God's best. Keep pressing on, don't give up and accept something that's second rate. There is abundant hope for you because God *is* the God of hope.

Consider the thief who hung on the cross next to Jesus. I'm sure he was being punished for some awful, murderous act. He was in physical, mental and spiritual misery, in absolute despair and hopelessness. But hanging there, he looked over at Jesus and somehow, seeing a glimmer of hope, he uttered these simple words, "Lord, remember me when you come into your kingdom." Jesus answered, "Today, you will be with Me in paradise." A few hours later, he was with Christ in paradise. It had been hopeless, but you see, it's never hopeless with God.

Think of Peter. Jesus was his dearest loved one and Master of whom he said, "I will die for You." Then Peter went out and denied the Lord three times. After his denials, he "wept convulsively" (Luke 22:62). He had no hope, he was despairing. Peter had no idea that Christ had future plans for him. He was going to be the one to launch the message of Christ to the rest of the world, reaching Jews and Gentiles alike. When Jesus rose from the dead, He appeared to Peter saying, "Buddy, I forgive you. Come on. Get back up now and strengthen your brothers. I'm strengthening you." Fifty days later, Peter was filled with the Holy Spirit. Through the Spirit's power, he became a completely different person. Before, Peter was so afraid, he couldn't even tell a simple little slave girl that he knew Christ. But then, having been filled with the Spirit fifty days later, he got up in front of thousands of people, gave a witness for Christ, and 3,000 of them gave their lives to Christ that day. What a fantastic transformation!

God's Part: Empowering

Romans 15:13 shows us that we like Peter are transformed by the power of the Holy Spirit, "Now may the God of hope fill you with all joy and peace in believing, that you may abound in hope by the power of the Holy Spirit." This verse can be broken down into two parts: God's part and our part. God's part is filling and empowering us "by the power of the Holy Spirit." It's not hard for this to happen. Jesus said, "If anyone is thirsty, let Him come to Me and drink of My Spirit. If you take Me up on My invitation continually, out of Your heart will overflow rivers of living water" (John 7:37-38).

First, you must be thirsty... you want more, you're not satisfied. Then, come to Christ and say, "Lord, fill my heart, overflow me." What will happen? Out of your heart will overflow rivers, turning you into a spiritual oasis in this desert world. The Lord wants to plant an oasis where you work, live, or go to school, so you can overflow and bless others. The only difference between brown, barren land and lush, green fields is irrigation. The only difference between a barren believer and an abundant believer is the Holy Spirit pouring in and the power of the Spirit filling and ruling our lives on a daily basis.

Our Part: Believing

"Now may the God of hope fill us with all joy and peace *in believing...*" When we repeatedly come thirsting to Christ to fill us, that's faith and that's believing. Believing is an active trust and dependency on God. We have a lot of terms these days about being "dependent." The Lord doesn't want you to be self-dependent or codependent, He wants you to be God-dependent. "For without faith, it is impossible to please God, for He who comes to God must believe that He is the ultimate reality and that He is a rewarder of those who seek after Him" (Hebrews 11:6).

Faith seeks after Him and faith honors God, because it believes God for who He is. For instance, faith means believing God is loving. When you're thinking, "God hates me," that's unbelief. Faith believes that God is gracious, God is merciful, God is compassionate, and God is sufficient and able. Faith honors God and God honors faith, and He blesses those who believe, even if we don't deserve it.

As we believe in Him, God helps us overcome all the barriers, stumbling blocks and attacks the world throws our way. "This is the victory that overcomes the world, even our faith" (1 John 5:4). Jesus Christ is the undefeatable victor and when your faith is latched on to Him, you've really got something! He wants to bring you into all that He has for you, because there is no limit to what He can do. The only limitation is in our unbelief.

Unbelief Versus Faith

Psalm 78:41 says Israel "limited the Holy One of Israel" through their unbelief. God wants to take you all the way into the Promised Land and then help you possess it. A person who doubts the Lord "is like a wave of the sea driven and tossed by the wind. For let not that man suppose that he will receive anything from the Lord; he is a double minded man, unstable in all his ways" (James 1:6-8). This means unbelief is a robber. Don't be ripped off. Believe God for His victory and overcoming power.

An old saint once said, "Doubt your doubts, and believe your beliefs." We have a tendency to believe our doubts and doubt our beliefs. Questions come along and immediately we start doubting. Why don't you doubt your doubts? When a doubt comes in say, "I doubt that!" If a skeptic challenges you, tell him, "I'm skeptical of you, skeptic!" Don't be skeptical of God and His promises, but be skeptical of the world's voices. There is a place for honest doubt, but over time, the Lord will prove Himself and show you His trustworthiness.

In John Bunyan's book *Come And Welcome To Jesus Christ,* he contrasts unbelief with faith:

• Faith sees more in a promise of God to help than in all other things to hinder; but unbelief, in spite of God's promise says, "How can these things be?"

• Faith will make you see love in the heart of Christ when with His mouth He gives correction, but unbelief will imagine wrath in His heart when with His mouth and word He says He loves us.

• Faith will help the soul to wait, when God delays to give, but unbelief will get impatient and angry if God makes any delays.

• Faith will give comfort in the midst of fears, but unbelief causes fears in the midst of comforts.

• Faith makes great burdens light, but unbelief makes light ones intolerably heavy.

• Faith helps us when we are down, but unbelief throws us down when we are up.

- Faith brings us near to God when we are far from Him, but unbelief puts us far from God when we are near to Him.

- Faith puts a man under grace, but unbelief holds him under wrath.

- Faith purifies the heart, but unbelief keeps it polluted and impure.

- Faith makes us see preciousness in Christ, but unbelief sees no form, beauty, or comeliness in Him.

- By faith we have our life in Christ's fullness, but by unbelief we are unfulfilled and waste away.

Do you see why faith makes the difference? When you do your part by simply believing Him, He will fill you. The baseball players in the movie *Field of Dreams* said, "Build it and we will come." Jesus is saying, "Believe Me, and I will fill." His will is abundance of Himself for you.

When Romans 15:13 declares, "abound in hope," the word "abound" means "waves upon waves." The Lord has an ocean of blessings from

Himself that He wants to give to each and every one of us. Those blessings come in all different kinds of waves: Some are soft, gentle waves; others are thrilling, exciting waves that you catch and surf on; some are hard, crushing waves, but even then, He gives you more of His grace, love, and mercy. In Him is found fullness of joy, peace and hope that no one can ever take away. He is the God of hope, and let me tell you, you're not hopeless! "Dear Lord Jesus, make us samples to others of your goodness, Your joy, and Your hope. Amen."

How to Become a Christian

First of all you must recognize that you are a sinner. Realize that you have missed the mark. This is true of each of us. We have deliberately crossed the line not once, but many times. The Bible says, *"All have sinned and fallen short of the glory of God"* (Romans 3:23). This is a hard admission for many to make, but if we are not willing to hear the bad news, we cannot appreciate and respond to the *good news*.

Second, we must realize that Jesus Christ died on the cross for us. Because of sin, God had to take drastic measures to reach us. So He came to this earth and walked here as a man. But Jesus was more than just a good man. He was the God-man—God incarnate—and that is why His death on the cross is so significant.

At the cross, God Himself—in the person of Jesus Christ—took our place and bore our sins. He paid for them and purchased our redemption.

Third, we must repent of our sin. God has commanded men everywhere to repent. Acts 3:19 states, *"Repent therefore and be converted, that your sins may be blotted out, so that times of refreshing may come from the presence of the Lord."* What does this word *repent* mean? It means to change direction–to hang a U-turn on the road of life. It means to stop living the kind of life we led previously and start living the kind of life outlined in the pages of the Bible. Now we must change and be willing to make a break with the past.

Fourth, we must receive Jesus Christ into our hearts and lives. Being a Christian is having God Himself take residence in our lives. John 1:12 tells us, *"But as many as received Him, to them He gave the right to become children of God."* We must receive Him. Jesus said, *"Behold, I stand at the door and knock. If anyone hears My voice and opens the door, I will come in..."* (Revelation 3:20). Each one of us must individually decide to open the door. How do we open it? Through prayer.

If you have never asked Jesus Christ to come into your life, you can do it right now. Here is a suggested prayer you might even pray.

Lord Jesus, I know that I am a sinner and I am sorry for my sin. I turn and repent of my sins right now. Thank You for dying on the cross for me and paying the price for my sin. Please come into my heart and life right now. Fill me with Your Holy Spirit and help me to be Your disciple. Thank You for forgiving me and coming into my life. Thank You that I am now a child of Yours and that I am going to heaven. In Jesus' name, I pray. Amen.

When you pray that prayer God will respond. You have made the right decision–the decision that will impact how you spend eternity. Now you will go to heaven, and in the meantime, find peace and the answers to your spiritual questions.

Taken from: *Life. Any Questions?*
by Greg Laurie, Copyright © 1995. Used by permission.

Other books available in this series...

Spiritual Warfare
by Brian Brodersen
Pastor Brian Brodersen of Calvary Chapel Westminster, England brings biblical balance and practical insight to the subject of spiritual warfare.

Christian Leadership
by Larry Taylor
Pastor Larry Taylor of the Cornerstone Christian Fellowship in Maui, Hawaii discusses the basics of leadership in the church and challenges us to become leaders that serve.

The Psychologizing of the Faith
by Bob Hoekstra
Pastor Bob Hoekstra of Living in Christ Ministries calls the church to leave the broken cisterns of human wisdom, and to return to the fountain of living water flowing from our wonderful counselor, Jesus Christ.

Practical Christian Living
by Wayne Taylor
Pastor Wayne Taylor of Calvary Fellowship in Seattle, Washington takes us through a study of Romans 12 and 13 showing us what practical Christian living is all about.

Building Godly Character
by Ray Bentley
Pastor Ray Bentley of Maranatha Chapel in San Diego, California takes us through a study in the life of David to show how God builds His character in our individual lives.

Worship and Music Ministry
by Rick Ryan & Dave Newton
Pastor Rick Ryan and Dave Newton of Calvary Chapel Santa Barbara, California give us solid biblical insight into the very important subjects of worship and ministering to the body of Christ through music.

Overcoming Sin & Enjoying God
by Danny Bond
Pastor Danny Bond of Pacific Hills Church in Aliso Viejo, California shows us, through practical principles, that it is possible to live in victory over sin and have constant fellowship with our loving God.

Answers for the Skeptic
by Scott Richards
Pastor Scott Richards of Calvary Fellowship in Tucson, Arizona shows us what to say when our faith is challenged, and how to answer the skeptic in a way that opens hearts to the love and truth of Jesus Christ.

Effective Prayer Life
by Chuck Smith
Pastor Chuck Smith of Calvary Chapel of Costa Mesa, California discusses the principles of prayer, the keys to having a dynamic prayer life, and the victorious results of such a life. It will stir in your heart a desire to "pray without ceasing."

Creation by Design
by Mark Eastman, M.D.
Mark Eastman, M.D., of Genesis Outreach in Temecula, California carefully examines and clarifies the evidence for a Creator God, and the reality of His relationship to mankind.

The Afterglow
by Henry Gainey

Pastor Henry Gainey of Calvary Chapel Thomasville, Georgia gives instruction in conducting and understanding the proper use of the gifts of the Holy Spirit in an "Afterglow Service."

Final Curtain
by Chuck Smith

Pastor Chuck Smith of Calvary Chapel Costa Mesa, California provides insight into God's prophetic plan and shows how current events are leading to the time when one climactic battle will usher in eternity.

For ordering information, please contact:
The Word For Today
P.O. Box 8000, Costa Mesa, CA 92628
(800) 272-WORD
Also, visit us on the Internet at:
www.thewordfortoday.org